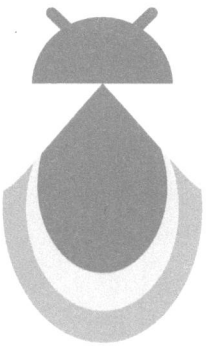

# Firefly
## Classrooms

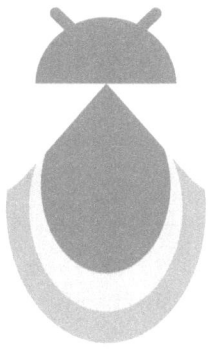

**10 ELEMENTS
OF AUTHENTIC TASKS
THAT MAKE LEARNING
VISIBLE AND SOCIAL**

# TROY COCKRUM

Firefly Classrooms
Copyright © 2018 by Troy Cockrum

All rights reserved. No part of this book may be reproduced or transmitted in any form or by any means without written permission from the author. For information regarding permission, contact the author at books@fireflyteacher.com.

This books is available at special discounts when purchased in quantity for use as premiums, promotions, fundraisers, book clubs, or for educational use. For inquiries and details, contact the publisher at books@fireflyteacher.com.

Published by Firefly Teacher Books
Indianapolis, IN
www.fireflyteacher.com

Cover and interior formatting by Mark Thomas / Coverness.com
Illustrations by Elie Heile and Ingrid Miller

Library of Congress Control Number 2018903267
Paperback ISBN 978-1-7321305-0-0
Ebook ISBN 978-1-7321305-1-7

First Printing: June 2018

# Praise for

# Firefly Classrooms:

"The **WE CAPTURED** acronym Troy shares can be applicable to problem-based learning projects, Genius Hour / 20% Time, or even daily learning we're asking of our students. Open the jar, get the students involved, and let them fly with the ten elements that make learning stick. The more elements teachers can apply, the more they can step back and see their students shine!"

-**Joy Kirr, author of** *Shift This!: How to Implement Gradual Changes for MASSIVE Impact in Your Classroom*

"Troy Cockrum has written a practical, applicable book to "capture" student learning and engagement. With his 11 years of classroom experience, this is NOT a theory book, but rather a guide to student centered learning and valuable, tested lessons. If you are interested in empowering your students for growth, collaboration, and social impact, then this is the book for you!"

    -**Don Wettrick, author of** *Pure Genius: Building a Culture of Innovation and Taking 20% Time to the Next Level*

"Troy's passion for education and for life shine through in *Firefly Classrooms*. He is able to break down the art of inspiring learning in children to very tangible and practical steps, essentially blurring the line between the art and the science of teaching. If you struggle to implement some of the inspiring concepts around authentic learning and are looking for some practical tips and examples of authentic learning, look no further. *Firefly Classrooms* has something for every educator and is certain to help both novice and veteran teachers improve their craft and engage students in ways they never have before."

    -**Aaron Sams, author of** *Flip Your Classroom: Reach Every Student in Every Class Every Day, Flipped Learning: Gateway to Student Engagement, Flipped Learning for Math Instruction, Flipped Learning for Science Instruction, Flipped Learning for Elementary Instruction, Flipped Learning for English Instruction,* **and** *Flipped Learning for Social Studies Instruction.*

"*Firefly Classrooms* and the authentic classroom experiences Cockrum shares provides teachers a path toward redefining learning and reaching the higher ordered thinking we all want to see out of our students."

   **-Kevin Brookhouser, author of** *The 20time Project* **and** *Code in Every Class*

# Table of Contents

Praise for ............................................................................................... 5

Firefly Classrooms: ............................................................................. 5

Foreword ................................................................................................ i

Preface - Capturing My Own Fireflies ............................................. v

Chapter 1 - Capturing Fireflies ......................................................... 1

Chapter 2 - Growing a Firefly Classroom ....................................... 8

Chapter 3 - Fireflies Adapt to Their World (W - Task has Real-World relevance) ............................................................................................. 20

Chapter 4 - Starring Fireflies (E - Task is Examined from different Perspectives) ........................................................................................ 38

Chapter 5 - If Fireflies Work Together, They All Have More Success (C - Task is Collaborative) ......................................................................... 57

Chapter 6 - Fireflies Need Support to Fly (A - Task is integrated Across different Subjects) ................................................................................ 70

Chapter 7 - The Light of a Firefly Is the Product (P - Task involves producing a Polished Product) .......................................................................................... *85*

Chapter 8 - Fireflies Accomplish a Lot in the Time Given (T - Task is sustained over a period of Time) .................................................................... *104*

Chapter 9 - Fireflies Decide What They Need to Learn (U - Task is Undefined requiring students to define the tasks) ......................................................... *119*

Chapter 10 - Fireflies Use Reflection to Maximize Their Light (R - Task requires Reflection) ..................................................................................... *130*

Chapter 11 - Fireflies Use All Necessary Skills to Communicate (E - Task Employs a seamless integration with assessment) ...................................... *149*

Chapter 12 - Firefly Diversity (D - Task has a Diversity of outcomes and competing solutions) ..................................................................................... *169*

Chapter 13 - Fireflies Are Captured, Not Delivered ................................... *183*

About the Author ......................................................................................... *187*

Hire Troy Cockrum! ..................................................................................... *189*

# Projects Index

Chapter 3

Cardboard Regatta ...................................................................................... *20*

Holiday Bazaar ............................................................................................ *29*

Chapter 4

Kiva Communities ...................................................................................... *39*

Oral Histories .............................................................................................. *46*

Chapter 5

Write a Book in a Day ................................................................................. *57*

Famous Hoosiers Wiki ................................................................................ *64*

Chapter 6

Design a Theme Park .................................................................................. *70*

Travel Blogs ................................................................................................. *79*

Chapter 7

Simple Machines ......................................................................................... *85*

Podcasting ................................................................................................... *92*

Chapter 8

Near Space Balloon Launch .......................................................................... *104*

Sphero Stories ................................................................................................ *112*

Chapter 9

20 Time/Genius Hour .................................................................................... *119*

Digital Museum ............................................................................................. *124*

Chapter 10

Create a Civilization ...................................................................................... *130*

Augmented Reality Planets . ......................................................................... *140*

Chapter 11

Mock Trial ...................................................................................................... *150*

Civil Rights Problem-Based Learning ......................................................... *157*

Chapter 12

Design 3D Objects . ........................................................................................ *169*

Service Videos ................................................................................................ *175*

# Foreword

A field full of fireflies is enough to make my day. (Or night.) There are plenty of them in the open fields and woods by my home in the middle of nowhere in west central Indiana. (Seriously, nowhere ... we have three neighbors in a mile radius of our house.) I've seen my own kids chase and try to capture fireflies. We've poked holes in the top of jars and watched them crawl around.

I wasn't sure what to make of Troy Cockrum's *Firefly Classrooms* when I heard the title at first. But the connection is perfect to the kind of learning our students crave and deserve. You'll love how he spells that out so effectively in Chapter 2. When learning takes the firefly model -- open the jar, ready the lids, close the jar -- students own their learning and it's truly authentic.

You'll appreciate Troy's descriptive writing style. Like a true wordsmith, he crafts stories that exemplify the ideas in his book. This book is far from the "theory without practice" titles you find in education. Troy has spent time in classrooms seeing the impact and results from firefly teaching. You'll be inspired and entertained by his stories and equipped to put them into practice.

Let's dig into *Firefly Classrooms* and bring some new light into teaching and learning!

**Matt Miller**

**Speaker, blogger and author of** *Ditch That Textbook*

# Preface

# Capturing My Own Fireflies

From July 2012 until May 2016, I co-hosted a podcast with Joan Brown called *Flipped Learning Remixed*. Due to time constraints in our schedules, we chose to end the podcast after 145 episodes and nearly four years. I wanted to keep producing the podcast, because I enjoyed the process of creating content for others. The process of researching a topic or preparing for an interview, figuring out how to obtain and upload the best quality audio and video, and making sure I was journalistically fair to the topic as a professional standard all appealed to me. For me, the polished product was important. Unfortunately, I was involved in too many other projects (including writing this book), so that Joan and I decided we weren't being fair to the process and the original intention of the podcast and chose to end it.

Along the way though, I was gaining valuable fireflies of knowledge about different education technology topics. This was a time when I really started to come together with the elements of **WE CAPTURED**. I was able to start to put into words an organized list of authentic learning.

In August 2014, I began my doctoral work at Indiana University. This allowed me the opportunity to take a step back as a classroom practitioner, even though I was still in the classroom, and to look at what research was available on authentic learning. The more I explored the research, the more these common elements that I was trying to put into words were emerging. Through a combination of my professional experience and research, the elements of **WE CAPTURED** were bouncing around in my head.

Then one day in December 2015, I stood in my office with a stack of Post-it notes and began sticking them all over the walls, writing words and phrases on them. Until finally, I was left with **WE CAPTURED**: the ten elements of authentic learning. My fireflies of learning had been posted all over my office walls until I could capture them into the structure of this book.

# Chapter 1

*Capturing Fireflies*

*What are Firefly Classrooms?*

"Mom, do we have a jar to catch fireflies?" asked one of my cousins to his mother.

Settling myself into a lawn chair, I was soaking in all the activity around me. I watched my aunts and uncles washing dishes, bagging up trash, and folding tablecloths. I watched others putting bug spray on their children and reminding them of responsible behavior as the sun was going down behind the trees. This was an annual dance my family played every year on the Saturday evening of our extended family reunion.

I smiled at the nostalgic memories of catching fireflies on a warm summer evening growing up in the midwest. Several of the kids cheered excitedly as Charlie's mom pulled out the jar she brought with her just for this occasion.

"Yes, but make sure you include everyone."

The children scampered around the campsite. The older

kids explained to the younger ones how to spot fireflies.

"Oh, there's one on your shoulder," a savvy adolescent said, pointing to her six-year-old cousin's shoulder. "Stay still and let me grab it."

She quickly cupped her hands around the firefly and gently trapped it between her palms. Pinching her thumbs together, she formed an opening at her knuckles to allow her younger cousins to view inside her hands.

"See it light up that green color?" she instructed.

The younger kids squealed with excitement at the novel display happening before their eyes.

Opening her hand, the girl revealed to the others what a firefly looked like when it wasn't glowing. The stunned firefly regained its senses and flew away.

At this point, all the adults had taken their spots around the fire and were conversing about all the family happenings. As the sun went down further and darkness came upon us, the children continued to chase after fireflies.

"I've got one," screamed one child. "Where's the jar?"

"Ohhhh, I missed it," hollered another.

The children started developing strategies based on their experiences. Even the cousins from out west, who had never seen a firefly light up until that night, were figuring out how to best catch the insect. Unbeknownst to them, the children started to discover the ideal conditions for firefly activity. A small stream trickled just beyond the campsite along a line of trees. Normally, the stream would be dry. But, due to the recent rainy weather, there was a marshy water bed in which fireflies thrive. The line of trees provided cover that fireflies tend to group under for their mating rituals. The children also discovered that flickering the bulb on their flashlights sometimes elicited an ember response from a firefly.

As the jar was filling up with active fireflies, the adults reminded the kids not to stray too far away. The children gathered around a nearby picnic table with the lighted jar as their centerpiece. Giggles of amazement spurred out from the young voices as they marveled at the wonder of a jar full of sparkling fireflies.

As I watched this all unfold, the kids using inquiry and teamwork to capture the fireflies, I realized this is what I wanted my classroom to look like. A band of students looking for sparks of knowledge and reaching out eagerly to capture and examine. That is a Firefly Classroom! But, just as fireflies, the conditions have to be right to be active. As educators, if we don't create the right environment, encouraging an active classroom, the fireflies of knowledge won't be there for our students to capture.

### Capture versus Deliver

I'm really bothered by the phrase "deliver a lesson." Why? Because "deliver" requires one side to be passive in the distribution of content. Our local pizza shop delivers a pizza.

The postman delivers a package. The word "deliver" implies one person bringing something to another person. In the case of delivering a lesson, the implication is that the teacher is the active party and the students are passive participants receiving information. As teachers, we shouldn't be considered the only source of knowledge for our students. They shouldn't passively sit back and expect us to *deliver* them knowledge. In order for them to capture that knowledge, they need to be active participants in the process. That passivity is ineffective for deeper learning and is an outdated view of education. Students should be as active, actually probably more active, than the teacher in their learning process.

Instead, I believe students should capture learning. The very act of capturing something requires active participation. It requires planning and problem-solving. Just like the kids grabbing fireflies. And, once they've captured that knowledge, they need to put what they grabbed in their "jars" to enjoy later.

> *"The very act of capturing something requires active participation. It requires planning and problem-solving."*

## The Need to Be Active and Authentic

In order for students to actively capture learning, the classroom has to be truly student-centered. To be truly student-centered, we need learning to be authentic. Creating an authentic learning environment isn't always easy, but it is imperative. Lev Vygotsky promoted the four main characteristics of social and constructivist learning as 1) the learner actively constructing his or her own knowledge, 2) that social interactions are important to knowledge construction, 3) self-regulation and metacognition play a crucial role in learning, and 4) the learning tasks are authentic. In today's world, where learners have a wealth of social opportunities, both global and local, at their fingertips, and communities of common interest are increasingly easier to find, these characteristics of learning couldn't be more true. Therefore, educators need to allow their students to be active, by having them interact with others, and to develop learning tasks that have the value of authenticity.

Authentic learning requires students to create real, usable, quality products in which they share openly. In his book *World Class Learners,* Yong Zhao said, "The model of product-oriented learning makes the creation of products the center of the learning experience." That is where the capturing happens.

## Confusion about Authentic Learning

Some might say "authentic learning" is simply real-world activities. That is only true to an extent. Authentic learning encapsulates more than that real-world component. And, really, what is real-world to a second grader? Some concepts are so complex as real-world incarnations that we can't expect our kids to grasp them right away.

David Jonassen, a leading researcher on authentic learning, defined authentic activities as tasks that have real world relevance and utility. In addition, they integrate seamlessly across the curriculum, they provide levels of complexity, and they allow students to select appropriate levels of difficulty or involvement in the task.

A classroom needs to have these tasks that look like real-world problems, needing real-world solutions. The tasks should meet multiple standards, be cross-curricular whenever possible, and provide students with a voice in the learning and choice in their involvement. That is what a Firefly Classroom looks like.

# Takeaways

### What's in the Jar?

- Learning is Captured, not delivered
- Learning needs to be authentic
- Authentic learning is more than simply real-world activities

While reading this book, I encourage you to be social with your own learning. Interact on Twitter or Instagram using #fireflyclass. Or join the Firefly Classroom group on Facebook. Each chapter will end with some questions to help spark ideas.

### Share your thoughts using #fireflyclass

- What are your thoughts on delivering versus capturing learning?
- How do you find a balance between delivering and capturing?

# Chapter 2

*Growing a Firefly Classroom*

Fred Newmann and Gary Wehlage proposed the Five Standards of Authentic Learning. If an activity, lesson, or project meets these five standards, it can be considered an authentic task. They are: Higher-Order Thinking Skills (HOTS), Required Depth of Knowledge, Having a Connection to the World beyond the Classroom, Creating Substantive Conversations by the Learners, and Having Social Support for Student Achievement.

*Fireflies Produce the Most Efficient Light in the World (Higher-Order Thinking)*

The light produced by fireflies is actually a complex chemical reaction between calcium, adenosine triphosphate, and a luciferin. Virtually no energy is wasted in the production of light. Oftentimes, educators waste a great deal of student energy on low-level tasks. Learning is more meaningful when it involved a complex relationship with high-order thinking.

Higher-Order Thinking, often known as HOTS, is a buzzword frequently heard in education. This concept is based on Bloom's taxonomy. Repeating simple facts is not higher-order. It is not an efficient way to make learning bright. That is remembering. Facts can be looked up easily. It is what the students are doing with that information that is important. To get to the higher levels of Bloom's, students need to be analyzing, creating, and reflecting. However, they don't necessarily need to be creating new content. They could be repurposing or remixing others' content. If students aren't doing higher-order processing, they aren't doing authentic learning.

*Fireflies Bury Their Eggs Deeper into the Soil*
*(Depth of Knowledge)*

---

Firefly eggs need moist soil to thrive. Therefore, in order to ensure the soil stays moist, fireflies will bury their eggs under layers of soil or mulch. Placing their eggs at a greater depth allows the most optimal conditions for the fireflies to grow.

Norman Webb developed this concept, Depth of Knowledge. The idea is that the deeper we dig into material the more complex the cognitive processing becomes. The moist soil in the depth of knowledge allows learning to grow. It may be more challenging to dig down to the better soil. However, it is worth it because that is where learning thrives. Ultimately, we want students to not just recall information, but to extend their thinking beyond the information.

## Get Out of the Jar
### (Connected to the World beyond the Classroom)

Fireflies can only survive in a jar, even properly cared for, for only a day or two. They need to get out and expand their social connections. The irony is that fireflies will not leave the habitat in which they were born. If it is paved for a parking lot or turned into a subdivision, they will not migrate from the area. Instead, they just die off and disappear from the area.

Like the fireflies that need to be social, students do also. Too many teachers forget that the learning extends beyond the four physical walls of their classrooms. Even teachers with good blended or online classes forget the importance of connecting their students with peers around the world. Social media has created amazing opportunities to reach out to many audiences. We need to be sharing our students' work. Even better, our students need to be sharing their own work. Not just with their parents. And certainly not just hanging work in the hallway. If students don't "migrate" to other areas, their brilliance disappears. If student work is good enough for the hallway, it is good enough to share with the world.

However, we shouldn't just be sharing their final products. We should be finding opportunities to collaborate with others outside our classroom. Students should be developing empathy for other cultures and other students. I had my seventh graders video chat with a teenager living in Syria. We also met with local Syrian refugees and researched their struggles.

A Firefly Classroom facilitates those connections. I had a project with second graders doing audio recordings of pen pal letters using VoiceThread[1] and sent them to a school in another state to respond. The students were learning about community and how others define their own community. While it wasn't worldwide, it certainly connected the second graders to students who were different than them. If there is no connection to the world beyond the classroom, then it is not authentic learning.

*Illuminating the Conversation*
*(Substantive Conversations by the Learners)*

Fireflies "light up" as a means of communication. The light they emit and the pattern they use is a Morse code of sorts. It is intended to find them a mate, and the glowing abdomen signals compatibility. As teachers, the conversations in our classrooms should be an illumination between the students.

If the person doing the most talking in the room is the teacher, learning is stifled. Students need to be having conversations with each other. And not just surface level conversations, but substantive. As they explore their own thoughts, they need to bounce those thoughts off others and articulate them. Knowledge isn't just a piece of information

---

1 http://troy-cockrum.com/2nd-grade-letters/

that must be read or told. Knowledge is constructed through those substantive conversations.

In a Firefly Classroom, discussion is a frequently used learning tool. No matter the age, get students practicing meaningful conversation. Give them sentence starters while they're learning. Online discussion boards are great for extending the learning, too. A conversation that starts in a physical space can be continued for days online. For older students, Twitter chats can be powerful for creating conversation around an event, say a presidential debate.

Where do you go to discuss a topic with like-minded people? Is it a library, a coffeehouse, a community meeting, or even the local pool? Or is it Twitter or Facebook? Provide the space to encourage students to find those same connections. For instance, I worked with eighth graders using the tool TodaysMeet to backchannel during an in-class discussion. The backchannel provided all students an opportunity to converse with others on many different levels simultaneously. Oftentimes the discussion in the backchannel was entirely different than the oral in-class discussion. If students aren't having those conversations as they build their knowledge, or if students aren't getting the opportunity to have those conversations, then it isn't authentic learning.

# FIREFLY CLASSROOMS

*Synchronizing the Flashes (Social Support for Student Achievement)*

---

Some species of fireflies actually sync their flashing lights. It is believed they do this to reduce visual clutter. When large amounts of male fireflies inhabit a certain area, it can be difficult for female fireflies to separate from the masses and find their mate. Therefore, the male fireflies synchronize their display. In fact, there is a section of the Great Smoky Mountains in Tennessee that shuttles in thousands of visitors annually to watch a massive synchronous firefly display every June.

Let's face it, learning is social. This is the reason physical schools will not go away anytime soon, if ever. Learners need others to build skills, explore content, and construct knowledge. Learning in a social setting is more rich and dynamic. That doesn't mean that self-directed learning isn't powerful. But even self-directed learning usually has students talking to others. Students need to know how to drive their own learning. Why do so many students turn to YouTube when they want to learn something new? Even if they don't realize it, it is the social aspect of exploring someone else's content that is an engaging starting point.

But it isn't just that learning is social that makes it authentic. In a Firefly Classroom, we need to provide an environment where the social structure supports the student. The teacher and student peers need to set high standards for each other.

Students must be encouraged but also feel safe to take risks. And there has to be mutual respect between learners and teachers. That means supporting participation no matter what the quality. Everyone needs to feel they contribute in some way. The Initiate-Response-Evaluate (IRE) model that is very common in many classrooms frequently does not provide that student support. In this model, many times only one students gets to respond and the teacher evaluates that response (correct or incorrect) before the other students can process and make their own evaluations. I often used the Peer Instruction model, developed by Eric Mazur, in which students argue their answers with each other and must collectively agree on the correct answer before eventually being told the actual correct answer (if there even is one). This gives students the opportunity to defend their thoughts and to work through their learning.

## The Secret to Catching Fireflies

Let me explain how this book works. The five standards I just covered are a good starting point. But we need to go deeper. Therefore, I've put together 10 elements of authentic tasks that break these standards down more. As the book progresses through the elements, I will give project examples that I have done in my class or developed with other teachers for their classes. The reason I chose projects in which I was personally involved is not necessarily because I think that I have all the best ideas, but rather, as Henry David Thoreau wrote in *Walden*: "I should not talk so much about myself if there were anybody else whom I knew as well. Unfortunately, I am confined to this theme by the narrowness of my experience."

Each project I talk about is built on the Firefly Model:

## ✸ FIREFLY MODEL

Open the Jar

Jars Open, Lids Ready

Closing the Jar

"Open the Jars" is the introduction stage of a lesson. It should have an engaging hook that is designed to get the students thinking and asking questions. "Jars Open, Lids Ready" is the stage of the lesson where students are doing the messy work of solving problems, collaborating, asking more questions and really finding their fireflies. "Closing the Jars" is the stage in which we really lock in the learning. It requires reflection and recapping the learning.

When I talk about student learning, I purposely chose the word "captured". "**WE CAPTURED**" is not just the concept of grabbing our learning, but it is also an acronym for my 10 Elements of Authentic Learning. The literature on blending learning consistently shows these elements as being essential in creating authentic learning activities: the kinds of activities that allow students to capture learning and not just accept delivery of it. Each of the following chapters will discuss in detail each of those elements.

The 10 elements are:

W - Task has Real-World relevance

E - Task is Examined from different Perspectives

C - Task is Collaborative

A - Task is integrated Across different Subjects

P - Task involves producing a Polished Product

T - Task is sustained over a period of Time

U - Task is Undefined requiring students to define the tasks

R - Task requires Reflection

E - Task Employs a seamless integration with assessment

D - Task has a Diversity of outcomes and competing solutions

Let me be clear, you don't necessarily have to meet all of these elements with every task or project. The more elements you can meet, the better. However, all the elements should appear across multiple domains (activities, tasks, projects, lessons) several times throughout a school year. The sample projects I have selected meet many of the elements, but I have placed each project under the element I believe it most strongly meets.

You'll also notice that the projects are in narrative form and not in step-by-step process. You could certainly take these projects and use them just as I did. But you should use your own creativity and expertise to develop similar projects that will meet the needs of your students. You have your own experiences that are valuable to this process. I want you to understand *why* you are doing the project. That is what will make them successful. Evaluate your own projects based on these elements and see if you can improve them to help your students capture learning. I want students to love learning. That's what **WE CAPTURED** is all about: putting your students in an environment where they can capture their fireflies of learning.

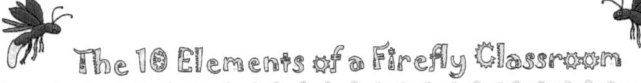

# The 10 Elements of a Firefly Classroom

W - Task has Real-World relevance

E - Task is Examined from different Perspectives

C - Task is Collaborative

A - Task is integrated Across different Subjects

P - Task involves producing a Polished Product

T - Task is sustained over a period of Time

U - Task is Undefined requiring students to define the tasks

R - Task requires Reflection

E - Task Employs a seamless integration with assessment

D - Task has a Diversity of outcomes and competing solutions

# Takeaways

### What's in the Jar?

- The Five Standards of Authentic Learning are: Higher-Order Thinking Skills (HOTS), Required Depth of Knowledge, Having a Connection to the World beyond the Classroom, Creating Substantive Conversations by the Learners, and Having Social Support for Student Achievement.
- If student work is good enough for the hallway, it is good enough to share with the world.
- **WE CAPTURED** is a way to remember the 10 elements of authentic learning.

### Share your thoughts using #fireflyclass

- Which element of **WE CAPTURED** excites you most?
- Which element of **WE CAPTURED** seems most challenging to you?

# Chapter 3

*Fireflies Adapt to Their World*

**W** - *Task has Real-**W**orld relevance*

*Fireflies Like Water*
___

"There is no way cardboard can float," exclaimed Olivia. The skeptical seventh grader wasn't convinced. "It will just soak through and fall apart."

"It is possible. Don't ask me exactly how, but I've seen YouTube videos of cardboard boats that actually float," I assured her.

"I just don't believe it," she huffed as she crossed her arms playfully, signalling the argument was over.

I had just explained to the seventh grade science class that we were going to be doing a cardboard regatta.

When I saw on Twitter that someone in California had done this with their class, I was intrigued. I went to our science teacher, Anita Navin, and said, "We have to do this."

She responded: "Maybe later in the year we can do boat prototypes. I don't think I know enough about boats and buoyancy and all that to actually teach them how to build a cardboard boat."

"Neither do I, but they'll figure it out," I said. "And if they don't, they'll still learn something in the process."

After more back-and-forth, I convinced Anita to allow me to do it.

The first problem I had to overcome was to find a place to host the regatta. If we were going to put cardboard boats large enough to support a person in the water, we needed a lake or a pool to host the event. Now, I'm in Indiana. There are plenty of lakes and pools that can be used in the warmer months. But this was January, and I wanted to plan the event for no later than March. So we needed an indoor pool. Well, it just so happened that one of the students in another grade at my school had a mother who worked at a nearby YMCA that had an indoor pool. Firefly teachers should always be making connections, because you never know when one will come in handy at a time like this.

Imagine this phone call, after exchanging pleasantries with the mother: "Hey, umm… I wanted to see if there was a time I could book your pool during the day?"

She laughed. "Sure?" she said quizzically and with a slight hesitation. "What for?"

"Well, I'm having the seventh graders build cardboard

boats, and I wanted to bring the boats by one day once they are complete and put them in the water. You know, to see how well they float and such."

"Oh, sure," she said excitedly. "I'd be glad to help."

She said she'd check the schedule and get back with me. We exchanged emails back and forth to hash out the details. I informed her we would need a lifeguard on duty, who would probably need to be in the water just to be safe. She responded, "Why is that?"

"Well, if (or, more likely, when) the boats sink, I want to make sure the kids are safe," I responded, thinking it was a reasonable request.

Her response was one question: "Wait… you mean the boats will be big enough for the kids to sit in?"

I'd find later that this was a common response when I told anyone about this project. It turns out that she was under the impression we were making boat prototypes, too. Firefly teachers think big!

## Fireflies Are Persistent

I then began researching parameters. Having no idea what materials would be advantageous to students, since I'd never built a cardboard boat, I decided the keep the rules very simple. Materials allowed: cardboard, duct tape, and paint (for decoration only). Challenge: at least one team member must be in the boat and propel it across the pool. That was it.

To give everyone a chance to excel, I decided to give awards for most functional (boat that traveled the farthest the fastest), most creative design, and most spirited team. I had no rubric, no criteria for grading these boats, just confidence that the students would run with this and make it a great experience. You see, confidence is important for Firefly teachers. Confidence that your students will put in the effort to complete the project no matter the difficulty. When you are overly restrictive in parameters, students feel as though they can't be trusted to complete a good project. Having that faith in their ability doesn't magically turn all students into diligent workers overnight. Some will still need some encouragement and support along the way. But nothing kills motivation more than being told exactly how to do something, allowing no personal autonomy for success or failure. Give your students a chance to surprise you!

# Lesson Elements

### Open the Jars

When I introduced it to the students, reactions were mixed. There were the skeptics, like Olivia, and there were others who were extremely excited to get started, and many in between. But all were intrigued. This class had 29 students, so I decided on six groups.

Week after week went by, and nearly every design was different. The conversations the students were having were amazing. I listened as one group had a lengthy argument about whether the weight of the person in the boat mattered. The person most excited to ride in the boat was not the lightest in the group. After some research, they realized the weight did matter, and they chose the lightest group member.

Some groups built their boats upward to allow them to float longer, but they moved more slowly. Others built their boats for speed, with little regard to how long they could stay afloat. I was truly surprised to see how many different designs the students came up with. And since I honestly didn't know how to build a boat out of any material, let alone cardboard, it was full inquiry by the students. We were all learning together. My answer to almost every question was: "I don't know. Try it and see."

## Jars Open, Lids Ready

The day of the regatta came. Even though it was a cold Friday in February and a fresh dusting of snow covered the ground, the kids were eager to put on their bathing suits and head to the pool. I loaded all the boats in a parent's van to transport them over to the pool. Every group had completed a boat that at least had a chance to float. A couple of them had cut the deadline a little close, and I wasn't sure they'd have a boat, but they still finished. Some would later realize that, in their haste to finish, they had made some poor decisions on the design. All of this was part of the learning process.

We turned many heads as we carried six cardboard boats into the YMCA, all different shapes and sizes, and headed toward the pool. Staff members from other areas of the fitness center wandered over to see what was going to happen. Many had their smartphones recording. It became an impromptu community event! Everyone seemed just as excited as the students.

After going over safety rules and lining the boats and students up along one side of the pool, it was time to launch.

The first boat was placed in the water, and Carlos gingerly was helped into the boat by his group mates. It was a sleek and narrow boat designed for speed. The students agreed that all groups would use the same kayak paddle for propulsion. I handed Carlos the kayak paddle and gave him some last minute encouragement. We pushed the boat away from the pool edge to rambunctious cheers. And… it immediately sank!

Yes, Carlos was not more than a foot from the edge of the pool, and the boat sank fast. I'll admit, my optimism was waning a bit. I glanced over at Anita with an oh-no-I-hope-this-doesn't-happen-to-everyone look, and she smiled back encouragingly. However, the students remained positive. They applauded the first group's effort and were optimistic that *their* boats would fair better. Their excitement renewed my optimism, too.

The second boat into the water was Olivia's group. I was so thrilled to see the person her group had chosen to be in the boat was Olivia herself! The most skeptical student at the beginning of the project was now the captain of her group's watercraft. This boat was more square than the other boats; however, their unique feature was that they had covered the bottom in empty water bottles. They had pillaged a few of the bottle recycle bins in the school hallway and had attached about 60 empty bottles to their boat to act as pontoons.

We placed the boat in the water. The group helped Olivia in, I handed her the paddle, and she was off. Olivia stroked the water furiously and started to make some progress at first. But a design flaw in the boat made the boat begin to take on water very quickly, and it sank after only going about five yards. In their rush to finish the boat on time, they had forgotten to make sure all the bottles had caps on them. Therefore, some of the bottles began filling with water and weighed down the boat. I began to wonder if Olivia was right. We had put two boats in the water and had made almost no progress.

The third boat's design was a combination of width for stability with some length for a bit of speed. This group was very confident they would be successful, even naming their boat "Eat My Bubbles." Their key design decision was to cover a lot of the boat in duct tape to seal off any porous spots. The boat was placed in the water, Paige, the pilot, was helped in, the paddle was handed over, and then she released.

From the start, this boat was different than the others. Paige was staying afloat. She paddled left, then steered right, and, although haphazardly, she was making progress. The spectators began to cheer louder. Paige reached the halfway point of the pool and seemed to be tiring. The lifeguard in the water moved closer to be prepared for Paige's evacuation. Then the other students started chanting: "Paige! Paige! Paige!" Soon, the parents and YMCA staff members joined in. The chanting enlivened the captain, and she began paddling again. This time, she seemed to have figured out how to steer a little better, and her boat was going straighter. And it happened! Their boat made it the entire length of the pool, about 40 yards, without taking on any water. Paige stepped into the boat from one side of the pool and stepped out on the other side without getting so much as a toe wet. All the students were ecstatic. I was ecstatic. *It was possible to float and steer a cardboard boat!*

## Closing the Jars

Once back at school, we had discussions on what worked and what didn't work. Groups shared with other groups what they had learned to make their boat successful. All the students had the chance to examine each boat's design and explore why it worked or didn't work.

I don't know if any of these students will become boat builders, but some may become engineers. They all will be problem solvers. And, using this real-world activity, they learned a lot about buoyancy, water displacement, and how objects float (or don't float). Even better, the students captured learning in a way they will never forget.

## Fireflies Lighting the Holidays

I was a couple of months into the year at a new school when the principal said to me, "We need your eighth graders to work the Holiday Bazaar in December, and you'll have to give up some class time for them to prepare." Any teacher knows that giving up class time means getting behind on instruction. We never seem to have enough time to cover everything as it is. This was an annual tradition that I certainly couldn't change at this point, so I fumed silently and accepted the inevitable. However, I decided to tie a project into the Holiday Bazaar in order to take advantage of the opportunity for some authentic learning.

# Lesson Elements

### Open the Jars

As I was thinking about real-world activities related to the holiday season, I was inundated, as we all are, by holiday advertisements. Then it hit me: Why not take advantage of this blatant consumerism and develop a real-world project from that? I decided that the eighth graders would do an advertising campaign.

The way the Holiday Bazaar worked at my school was all the students in the school participated in making some holiday crafts as part of their art class. We had bracelets, scarves, blankets, ornaments, and more made by all the grades kindergarten through eighth. The eighth graders would supervise the production of these crafts and then man a table of crafts on the day of the Bazaar. A few days before winter break, the gym would be turned into a makeshift shopping mall where kids, parents, and community members could buy gifts and crafts for their families or themselves. The eighth graders were in charge because all the proceeds went toward the annual eighth grade class trip at the end of the school year.

The project I designed was kept to simple parameters. The students would create an advertising campaign for their crafts and signage for their table. However, to avoid the downsides of competition, I built in incentives that benefited everyone so that no one group felt the need to "sabotage" another group. We didn't want political ads!

### Jars Open, Lids Ready

In the weeks leading up to the Bazaar, the students learned about different media and how advertising works, we discussed copywriting and ad production, and we learned a lot about persuasion. Students watched different television commercials and determined their appeal. The groups assigned each member roles and decided what was the best way to reach their target audience. Instead of doing your traditional persuasive essay, the students were learning about persuasion in a real-world context… advertising.

All the groups made posters for the hallways; some even had testimonials. The posters were plastered around the school promoting a community event. Some groups made short TV commercials and asked other teachers if they could show the videos to their classes. I required students to get permission from the principal and other affected teachers before producing anything. This allowed them to learn what is intrusive to their audience. It was a good opportunity to discuss national advertising restrictions in the real world.

The amount of collaboration, not only within groups but between groups, was amazing. I had the opportunity to

> "Firefly teaching allows teachers and students the opportunity to explore extra content that is pertinent to the project because of the real-world applicability, but which may have never been discovered otherwise."

explain the Nash equilibrium (as explained in a video by Jac de Haan[2]). This is something that would make no sense to eighth graders except in a real-world context and really is not part of eighth grade standards. Firefly teaching allows teachers and students the opportunity to explore extra content that is pertinent to the project because of the real-world applicability, but which may have never been discovered otherwise.

This final event wasn't as angst-ridden as the regatta, because the students had completed several parts of the project in the weeks leading up to the event. Just like in the real-world, some projects have many evaluated steps along the way to completion to ensure a successful final product, whereas others require a great deal of self-evaluation to get to the final product. The kids scuttled around with excitement, drawing attention to their products.

"Who are you looking to buy a gift for?" Marcus showed

---

2 https://www.youtube.com/watch?v=jILgxeNBK_8

his true used-car-salesman side (I say that endearingly), connecting with each customer and trying to meet their needs.

"My mom," the tentative first grader muttered.

"Great, we have lots of things your mom would love." Marcus locked in on the sale while still making sure the children didn't overspend for something that didn't meet their needs.

Across the gym, George was showing his flair for entertainment. Dressed in a holiday outfit of green and red with a Santa hat, he danced and sang with the kindergartners to get them in the spirit. The students were overwhelmed with all the different directions they could go, but watching George sing and dance gave them a fun distraction to occupy their attention, which gave their teachers time to sort and direct them. That's where students like Caroline stepped up and offered to take several young students by the hand and guide them around the Bazaar.

Savannah got to show her leadership skills by coordinating her group's outfits and team spirit. She organized and managed their roles expertly and respectfully. She made sure every job was being performed, and she filled in wherever needed. Her group was humming along efficiently because of her leadership. Erin, another in her group, used her artistic talents to make beautiful signage around their display. Students were having fun and, in turn, everyone had fun

Even more importantly, students got to use their unique

skills to make the group successful. Every student felt like a valuable contributor. It really turned out to be quite a successful Holiday Bazaar, and the whole project helped the students capture many different elements of persuasion.

### Closing the Jars

After the Bazaar was cleaned up and all groups had sold out, we returned to the classroom to discuss our day. Students were very complimentary of each display. We recapped the different types of persuasion used throughout the process. Some had appealed to emotion in their product pitches, while others appealed to need or reason. In the end, the fireflies of learning lit up the holidays in so many ways.

## Fireflies' Purpose

Fireflies light up for a purpose, dictated by their real-world needs. Firefly Learning thrives in real-world situations.

You've just read about two projects that encapsulated real-world relevance. When I am looking to do a project that has real-world relevance, the first question I ask is, "Where is this skill seen in the real world?" That might seem like a simple question, until you start trying to break down activities for your students. I looked at persuasion and saw a connection to advertising. I looked at problem solving and saw a connection to boat building. If you want your students to learn more about World War II, maybe you have them design a monument that pays homage to some historical elements to the war. If you want students to learn about velocity, maybe they design a roller coaster.

One of the great things about the cardboard regatta is that it focused on process. Students need to learn that process is just as important as the final product. A common phrase in my room is, "The product is not the project." Students need to trust the process of constant problem solving, reviewing, iterating, revising, and finishing the project, which leads to better, more valuable work. As a writer, I know the value of the writing process from experience. Designing projects that help students get that experience is important. Finding ways to tie projects into real-world experiences is a big first step into authentic learning and a way to help students capture their fireflies of knowledge.

# Takeaways

### What's in the Jar?

- Firefly teachers show confidence in their students.
- Firefly teaching can create community events even when not planning to.
- Firefly teachers are adaptive.
- Firefly teaching allows teachers and students the opportunity to explore extra content.
- Students need to learn that process is just as important as the final product.

### #fireflyclass

- What are your struggles with finding real world relevance?
- What's one thing you've done that really captured real world relevance?

# Chapter 4

*Starring Fireflies*

***E**  -  Task is **E**xamined from different perspectives*

*Firefly Perspectives*

There are actually thousands of different species of fireflies. The species of fireflies in each community is determined by their adaptations to that environment. In some areas of South America, for instance, fireflies can be mistaken for stars by visitors because they fly a bit higher and remain illuminated longer. The local residents, however, rarely mistake them for stars. It comes down to perspective. The locals are accustomed to seeing that type of firefly, while someone from a community with different fireflies hasn't seen this type of display. The perspective with which we grow up becomes our reality. The fireflies don't know your reality. To understand them, however, is to understand the locals' perspective.

Learning, for our students, is very similar. Their learning

is affected by the perspective with which they grew up. Some students will have short sparks of learning they need to grab quickly, while others will have a longer illuminance, but they may need to reach a little higher. Therefore, a Firefly Classroom must examine tasks from a variety of perspectives to fully lock in learning.

## Fireflies as Community

"You can't get to Africa without a car. You'd have to throw stones down to walk across the water," said Ashley, a very confident second grader.

Jenny Johnson, the second grade teacher, had told me her students had little concept of distance. She was trying to teach them about communities: what makes a community, how a community grows, and what makes it unique. They've had many cultural lessons and understood that people from China, for instance, were different culturally from Americans. But, from their perspective, China was just around the corner. Being in a lower income neighborhood, many of these students hadn't traveled much, if at all. But, even if they had, I'm not sure if that would have helped them understand a world of communities. Which is why little Ashley believed she could throw down rocks and walk to Africa.

As Jenny and I talked, we didn't just want them to know people in another country were culturally different; we wanted them to understand a community from the perspective of someone living in that community. My first thought was to do a video call with someone in another country. The problem we ran into was many of the communities we wanted the students to connect with were on a significant time difference. Therefore, to have a live chat, one school would have to connect before or after school hours. Not an ideal situation. So, we decided instead to build our project using Kiva.org.

# Lesson Elements

### Open the Jar

Kiva bills itself as a microlending site that connects lenders to borrowers around the world. Microlending is a process where multiple contributors loan small amounts and collectively fund one loan. Kiva's mission is "to connect people through lending to alleviate poverty." They work in 80 different countries to invest in local people to help build their communities.

Before we turned the students loose to do a lot research on communities, we wanted the students to really think about how the communities were different and why. I reached out to my friend Shannon O'Donnell for help. Shannon is a round-the-world traveler, blogger[3], and author of *The Volunteer Traveler's Handbook*. She does a lot of work in helping travelers connect with local community organizations in need of their time and talents. Shannon just happened to be in the U.S. at the time, so she agreed to do a Google Hangout[4] with our budding lenders and give them some perspective from a person who has volunteered in many communities around the world. We prepped the students the day before so they would have questions ready. Shannon fielded questions about everything

---

3 alittleadrift.com
4 https://www.youtube.com/watch?v=xvjYvne0FNA

from the busiest cities she visited, to her favorite countries, and what she eats when she travels, among others.

After the chat with Shannon, Jenny and I had a discussion with the second graders and told them our plan. The class was going to add funds to a loan. But, first, they were going to explore the communities the loan would benefit and vote on which loan the class would fund. We asked the class if they would be willing to bring in $1 each. We certainly communicated with the parents that this wasn't a requirement, but a request. Every student willingingly brought in $1, and we collected $25 toward what would be our first loan.

Jenny and I then browsed through many of the loan requests, looking for communities we wanted the students to explore. We also focused on loans that had a higher probability to be funded soon and on ones that focused on different aspects of the communities in which they served. In the end, we chose five loan requests to present to the students. We had: a man in the Philippines who requested a loan for supplies to build his fishing business; a woman in Kenya who wanted a dairy cow to provide low-cost milk to her community; a man in El Salvador who was hoping to build a wash station for vegetables that he sold and to add electricity to his farmhouse; a woman in Ecuador who wanted to buy pigs to raise; and a man in Indonesia who was going to buy mobile phone minutes to build his inventory to resell to the local community. There were so many more we could have chosen, but we had to limit the number for the students. We presented them to the students and let their thoughts begin to ruminate.

### Open Jars, Lids Ready

Next, we asked the students to research the different communities. We gave them a series of questions to consider as they were learning about the community the loan would serve. The goal was to have each group explain to the class what they learned about the community and also to make a pitch on why their loan should be selected. The students were not only getting the opportunity to research and learn about different communities, they also were developing persuasive arguments to support their loanee. Even though these were second graders, their questions to each other as they researched were insightful.

"We should chose her because she's a girl. She'll be able to help her family," one girl said.

"It doesn't matter if she's a girl or boy. The boys have to help their families, too," responded another.

This dialogue led to some good discussion about if gender should matter in choosing the loan recipient. We also had discussions about why the person was asking for their specific need. For instance, a dairy cow to provide milk for a community was unusual for these students. For them, inexpensive milk is just up the road at the grocery store. So Jenny and I talked to them about why the other community may not have milk readily available at their nearest market. Students were beginning to grasp why these loans were important to those specific communities. The problem required them to view it from many perspectives and challenged their own perspectives. At the end of their research, they pitched to each other reasons why their community's loan should be funded, and the students voted. Again, students not only saw the different communities' perspectives, but also their classmates' perspectives and how they approached the problem.

## Closing the Jars

In the end, the Kenyan dairy cow was chosen. A discussion and reflection naturally led out of the vote. Students were eager to share their perspective and their learning.

Delaney asked, "Can we call or visit Agnes (the name of the Kenyan woman)?" That led to another discussion about distance, time, and travel costs.

Throughout the rest of the school year, students would often ask me about Agnes. More importantly, they got a better sense of what makes a community, and they actually developed pride in the community they had researched, as though they were part of that community.

This project was used specifically to help second graders understand what makes a community by exploring it from different perspectives. Certainly this goes well beyond the content traditionally covered in a textbook. While the history of communities is important for understanding them, all the historical information could be discovered through research and discussion. A Firefly teacher could certainly scale this up in complexity to work with older grades to see fireflies from a different perspective. These second graders only saw their own community fireflies before the lesson, but, after the lesson, they saw fireflies that looked like stars.

## Stories Are Created from Capturing Fireflies

"Did you know my uncle and my dad almost burned down the school?" Gina, a seventh grader, asked me. She definitely caught my attention, so I asked for more details.

"Yeah, when they went to school here, they accidently set fire to the church behind the school, and it burned down," she said, smiling. "Luckily, the fire department stopped the fire from spreading to the school and burning it down, too." I looked around at the other students to see if Gina was telling the truth. She was not normally a student to be dishonest or even joke around, but the story just sounded so unbelievable. Many of the other students had heard the story before and confirmed its accuracy.

Gina was a bit unclear on the details, but believed it had to do with a dropped candle.

"Sandy, Gina told me this unreal story today," I said to Sandy, a teacher who had been at the school for over 30 years.

"Yes," she giggled in anticipation of this story.

"She said her dad burned down the church next door and almost the school?"

Sandy laughed as if remembering a very fond memory.

"Yes, yes, he did!" She then proceeded to fill me on the details Gina could not provide.

This wasn't the first time I had heard some intriguing stories about the alumni of the school. Children had filled the hallways for close to 60 years, and many of the alumni still lived in the community. *What if we could collect many of these stories and preserve them for future students?* I thought. Oral histories is part of eighth grade standards. I decided we could produce our own oral history of the school and publish it.

# Lesson Elements

### Open the Jars

Before we got deep into the unit, I had each eighth grader identify different alumni that they could interview. To encourage students to really go back in time, I offered bonus points for the oldest alumni contacted. One student was able to find the oldest alumni that we could confirm was still living, who had graduated from the third class in the school's history, in 1944. Once they identified one or two people, those were submitted to me. As a class, we discussed ways to make sure we had a good deal of diversity. We needed alumni from different decades. We needed a good representation of gender and race to reflect the makeup of the school. We also wanted interviewees who attended during major historical events in the school's history. For instance, the school embraced integration several years before Brown vs. Board of Education and continued to promote diversity for several years after. Therefore, the students believed (and, of course, I agreed) that we should have some alumni from that time speak specifically to what that meant to them. The students really grasped the idea of examining different perspectives to tell a more complete story. Once the interviewees were selected and assigned, the students got busy scheduling their interviews.

## Jars Open, Lids Ready

Before the interviews started, I had the students examine different oral histories. They researched books and videos, and we identified the common elements to making a good oral history narrative. These elements were used by the students to generate a series of questions that could be good to ask each interviewee. Students didn't have to use those questions and were encouraged to write some of their own, but the questions served as a guide. It was important that all this was student-explored and student-generated. I could have simply given them a handout of questions to ask, but it wouldn't have captured the learning as well. They came up with many of the same questions I would have given them, but, by coming up with them on their own, they understood the importance of the questions.

Some students were able to do their interviews in person. I showed them some recording techniques and note-taking skills to make sure they captured everything from the interview so they could easily refer back to it when writing. Some students did their interviews over the phone, and some needed to do their interviews via email. This allowed us to discuss the advantages and disadvantages of each method. After the students completed the interviews, we had many small group discussions on what were the high points that might develop into an engaging narrative. Students asked questions of each other and pointed out nuggets of interest in each person's story. Some students realized they needed to go back to the alumni to ask more questions. Then each student went to writing.

As the writing process took place in the classroom, students regularly consulted with each other and with me to make revisions or share information.

"I realize that we have more in common than I thought we ever did," said Grace, referring to her interviewee as she shared with me the highlights of her interview.

She wasn't the only student discovering things about their interviewee and themselves. George wrote, "Not only was the school diverse, but it also had high standards for social justice and civil rights." He then told a story about how many students from the school, including his alumnus, boycotted a nearby swimming pool because it was not integrated. This was a pool most of the current students visited frequently during the summer, and they were surprised to learn this. This led the group to a very powerful discussion about whether they would take part in a boycott under similar circumstances. They weren't learning about civil rights from a textbook or story from some far away place. They were learning about how civil rights affected their own neighborhood and, for some of them, their own families.

Grace wrote: "'You are put on this Earth to help other people and if that means you have to sacrifice yourself to do it, then you should,' Ellen said. This quote stood out to me during the interview. I think it is one of wisdom and inspiration and represents a way of life everyone should take part in." She realized the important role of oral histories for teaching community values.

"It made me proud to come to this school," wrote Larry.

And Caroline summed up the project best, "Although the days of rootbeer floats and diners may not be here anymore, the memories of the people who were there live on."

Students need to see their voice, their perspective, being put out into the world for anyone to read or view, and not just their teacher.

## Closing the Jars

At the end of the writing process, I packaged each narrative into a book format, and we self-published through Lulu.com[5]. Self-publishing options have improved a lot since even 2009 when I did this project, so Firefly teachers should really embrace the medium. Students need to see their voice, their perspective, being out in the world for anyone to read or view, and not just their teacher. Rushton Hurley, author of *Making Your School Something Special: Enhance Learning, Build Confidence, and Foster Success at Every Level*, said: "If students are sharing their work with the world, they want it to be good. If they're just sharing it with you, they want it to be good enough."

The whole goal of the oral history book was not only to learn about oral histories, but also to examine a historical narrative from many perspectives. The alumni's perspectives were vital to the story as well as to current students' perspectives.

## Reopening the Jar

The following school year, I wanted to advance this project a little further. One thing that bothered me about the previous project you just read about was that even though it was oral traditions we were exploring, we had published a book. This helped them learn a lot about storytelling and synthesizing

---

5 http://www.lulu.com/shop/2008-2009-eighth-grade-class/an-oral-history-of-st-thomas-aquinas/paperback/product-4385739.html

those stories into writing. However, with new technologies continuing to evolve the storytelling space, I wanted the students to explore more modern versions of oral storytelling.

Arguably, gone are the days of the radio broadcast. However, I had been exploring this somewhat-new medium becoming progressively more popular, called podcasting. Podcasts can be thought of as modern day radio shows. This seemed like a great way to use digital media and examine oral histories. I decided we would record the audio from all the interviews and edit them into a podcast format.

At that time, I had never produced a podcast myself, so I was learning along with the students. We also weren't 1:1 with devices, so we had to either use the school laptop cart or the students' personal devices. I can't think of many more disappointing ends to a good project than to have the students hard at work to produce the final product and, due to an oversight on my part, they can't finish it. Maybe the tool doesn't allow them to share a video with others after they've recorded, maybe there is a time limit on the recording, maybe a tool conflicts with another tool you are trying to use; all these I've had happen to me and risked ruining a great project.

The students chose to use Audacity to record and edit their podcast. Audacity is a free, open-source audio editor that is very versatile and easy to use, especially for student use. I discussed music usages and copyright with students so they knew to respect others' creative content. I believe if we want students to become responsible creators of original content, they must learn to respect others' content.

After determining the tools, we went into the oral history research and an interviewee selection process very similar to the previous year. Everything progressed well, and all the students were able to produce an audio podcast about their alumni. The important thing was for the students to capture all the fireflies of learning in these projects; they needed to examine the content from different perspectives.

*Task is Examined from different perspectives - Starring Fireflies*

---

It is increasingly easier to connect with people around the world. Using technology resources to examine a task from different perspectives is valuable in helping students discover learning opportunities. Taking into consideration the perspective of others really helped enrich the projects and improved the quality of the final product. The students learned a valuable lesson in seeing the reality of others and the importance of that to their learning.

I can't underestimate the value of empathy. Being able to empathise with someone else's perspective when addressing a problem is a wonderful skill to help solve a problem. Sometimes the solution to the problem is just to understand someone else better. In both projects, not only did each student choose a different way to get to the final product, they also had the chance to examine how other people's perspectives can change their own viewpoints. One project was international in nature to understand a far away culture, while the other project was hyperlocal to understand their own history. We need to give our students the opportunity to examine a task from different perspectives in order to find a good solution, but, more importantly, to also learn more deeply from that solution. Discovering how others capture fireflies makes students better at capturing their own fireflies.

# Takeaways

### What's in the Jar?

- Others' perspectives help us tell the difference between fireflies and stars.
- Students need to see their voice, their perspective, being out in the world for anyone to read or view, and not just for their teachers.
- Firefly teachers should always be looking to expand and improve their projects.

### #fireflyclass

- What ways have you helped students examine others' perspective?
- What perspective do your students bring to learning that can be valuable?

# Chapter 5

*If Fireflies Work Together, They All Have More Success*

**C** - *Task is* **C**ollaborative

*Firefly Writing*
___

"You can't have a love triangle in one scene if it hasn't been in the whole story," Isabelle, a fifth grader, said demonstratively.

The class laughed uproariously.

"Yeah, we need to take that out," Anna said with a smile.

"Ok, Chapter 5… make note of that," I said as I motioned to the group representing Chapter 5.

This was the kind of discussion the fifth graders were having all day during our Write a Book in a Day project. Kristin Denni had let me take over her fifth grade class for an entire day with the goal of writing and publishing a book all in the same day. The concept was simple, but would require a great deal of collaboration from all to pull it off.

### Open the Jars

We started the day by deciding some of the very basic information.

"What are the two main types of books?" I asked.

"Real and made up," said Adam. "But I can't remember which is fiction."

"Yes, fiction is fake, and nonfiction is real. So the first thing we need to decide is do we want to write a fictional story or a nonfiction book?"

A quick vote was taken, and the students decided on fiction. A consensus selection made the vote easy, and no one was disappointed. Things were looking good!

Our next choice was genre.

"What is a genre?" I asked.

"Mystery!" shouted Jacob.

"Yes, mystery is a *type* of genre, but what does the word mean?"

"Genre," Anna paused, "am I saying that right?" I nodded approval as she continued. "Genre is like a category or style of a book."

"Yes, Anna. Good work."

The students began discussing their favorites and began shouting them out with excitement.

"Adventure," said Maia.

"Sci-fi," piped Vanessa.

"Mystery," reiterated Jacob.

"Western?" shouted Christina quizzically to the confusion of all the others. The class giggled at the thought of writing a western.

Kristin furiously wrote the genres on the whiteboard as the students added more. She and I added a couple more they hadn't thought to include, like historical fiction, realistic fiction, and even teen-oriented. This vote wasn't quite the overwhelming majority we had for the first vote, but most students were excited to write an adventure story, with some elements of mystery or intrigue. So that's what we went with: a mysterious adventure.

## Jars Open, Lids Ready

Now we were into the meat of the book. We had a genre and type and now needed to formulate a story. After some discussion, we chose to determine setting first. We fielded many suggestions.

"A playground," suggested Makayla.

"A haunted playground," added Adam to verbal gasps of intrigue from his classmates.

"An island," Faye threw out.

"What kind of island?" I asked.

"A tropical island?" she muttered.

"That works!"

"Mars," screamed out Jacob, trying desperately to turn the book into the sci-fi novel that he wanted. The class grumbled. Kristin wrote it on the board anyway. We reminded the students: "All suggestions are good suggestions. We don't judge at this point."

"OK, one more suggestion."

"A bathroom… no, a porta potty," shrieked Vanessa.

And those were our suggestions. The class debated the merits of each. They determined it would be difficult to write a whole novel *inside* a portable restroom, but I assured them if they were creative enough, they could do it. They also determined that Mars was a bit too sci-fi. So the voting came down to a tropical island and a playground (possibly haunted). And the island won.

We went through the process of deciding the number of characters and their names, and that is when the discussions started getting more heated. The more details we started to flesh out, the more divided the opinions became.

"This is a creative process for the entire group," Kristin encouraged the group. "No matter what decisions are made, we have to accept them and give up on our own ideas and go with the others to make it the group's best work."

Some students stubbornly suggested they could break from the group and write their own book. While some teachers might panic in this situation, Kristin handled it masterfully.

"You're welcome to do that, but you'll need to go work in

the hallway so you don't distract the group. We'd love to have you stay, though, and contribute your talent to the group."

The students stewed for a moment, then agreed to stay. We coached the students from early in the process on how to manage disappointment. By midday, all students seemed to have forgotten their disappointments and were actively involved in shaping the direction of the story.

It was time to make our plot fit into the elements of a story and to generate our outline. The students discussed different plot points they wanted to see their three characters, Brittany, Chloe, and Jeff, go through on this island.

Kristin divided the students into groups of three, and we assigned each group a chapter of the book. The students quickly adopted a system of "runners" from each group, who scurried around the room (and hallway) to ask different groups questions or to make requests.

I was thrilled and surprised at how deep the conversations went into what should and should not be in a story. Students had to defend to each other why their choices would make the story better. The whole process of collaborating forced them to really examine the elements of a good story, while at the same time defending their position or realizing they might be wrong and should reconsider their position.

"You can't kill Jeff that early in the story. He's a good guy; he deserves to go farther in the story," said Adam when he heard a group had written Jeff's untimely death into their chapter.

"Wow!" Vanessa said to her group. "Brittany is being really mean to Chloe. Shouldn't she be a little nicer?"

The students had some previous exposure to peer editing, but Kristin and I guided them with questions to consider. We wanted them to focus on content specifically and not grammar edits. Those would come later.

The groups hovered back over their computers to make the revisions necessary to complete the story. Referring to their feedback notes and the notes of others, love triangles were removed, more description was added in sections for clarity, dialogue was added or revised to give the characters a distinct voice, and the final story was taking shape.

After the revisions were made, each group shared their chapter with a different group. That group would then revise the mechanics of the chapter: spelling, grammar, punctuation, etc. And, with that, the final book was completed shortly before dismissal.

## Closing the Jars

Well, technically, we didn't finish in one day. I wanted the process to be just like it was for any other published author and to let the students face all the choices an author might need to make. Some production elements and a title needed to be determined. So the the next day I would meet briefly with the students to put the finishing touches on this book.

I published the book with a self-publishing tool provided by a major book seller. I mentioned in the last chapter that I had previously used Lulu, but, this being several years later, this platform had really made major improvements to the self-publishing route.

The students reviewed the cover choices and voted on the one with sort of a rocky beach scene, but with dark colors to fit the ominous story. I had the self-publishing site displayed on the interactive whiteboard so students could see all the different choices we needed to make. We had to choose a book size. Some students pulled out their rulers and drew out the sizes on a piece of paper to physically compare them. We also had to decide if we wanted glossy or matte finish… and we had a quick art lesson. Some students went over to Kristin's classroom library of books and began looking at all the different titles. It turned out, at least from their research on that one day in that one classroom library, that most teen books are glossy. So glossy it was.

And, with that, the fifth grade authors were ready to put their book to press. Within a few days, I was able to bring to the students a book, concepted, written, and edited by them through the course of one pressured-filled day[6]. Their proud smiles showed me the fireflies were captured and the project was a success.

---

6 http://troy-cockrum.com/brittany-and-the-beast/

## Fireflies Give Kids Multiple Chance to Grab Them

Collaboration within a class is great, but even more powerful can be collaborating with another class or group of peers. That's what we did when I was asked by a fourth grade teacher to help develop a collaborative assignment integrating technology.

Every fourth grader in the state of Indiana has to learn about famous Hoosiers. Therefore, if you do a Google search for "famous Hoosiers projects," there are pages of them from which to choose. After examining several, I found they were all very similar and none that really met our needs. We wanted the students to learn the importance of accuracy in research, how to collaboratively build knowledge, and, of course, to learn about some famous Hoosiers. What we came up with was a collaborative website.

# Lesson Elements

### Open the Jars

"Should my aunt send her dog to this island?" I asked the students after giving them time to review the website thedogisland.com. In other classes, I've used allaboutexplorers.com and the Save the Pacific Northwest Tree Octopus website[7], all websites with false information designed to fool readers. As we discussed the information on the websites, the students realize how unreliable even an official-looking website can be. We talked about the responsibility they have in providing quality, factual information on their famous Hoosier.

### Jars Open, Lids Ready

Using social media, I generated interest from teachers willing to participate with us. I created a Wiki website and shared it with all the teachers participating. There is a wealth of Firefly teachers on social media willing to jump into projects with me or to include me in part of their own creative projects.

Each student in each class was assigned a famous Hoosier and had to create an entry on the website for their famous person. We really stressed to the students the importance in

---

7 http://zapatopi.net/treeoctopus/

putting accurate, non-plagiarized information onto the site.

### Closing the Jars

At the same time, other students at different schools doing the same project could edit each entry for accuracy and add more details if necessary. They also added their own famous Hoosier, which other students could help them edit. The goal, we told the students, was to have a dynamic, reliable resource for all fourth graders across the state to learn about more famous Hoosiers. Our goal was really for them to collaborate on this site with peers from other schools in other cities and also to learn the importance of accurate research.

As the students read about Larry Bird and Jim Davis (two of the most popularly chosen famous Hoosiers) and saw their peers work on other famous Hoosiers, you could see the fireflies sparkling in their eyes.

## If Fireflies Work Together, They All Have More Success

When I think of collaboration, I look at ways the group can build not only a project, but also build knowledge for the collective good. Everyone should benefit from the interaction of the group involved. Some people mistake collaboration for everyone giving equal participation in a project, but that is not authentic. Everyone brings different skills or experiences that can be contributed. Some people mistakenly believe that fireflies don't exist in the western United States. The fact is, however, that they do. The reason people believe they don't exist is because their luminosity is so faint to the human eye, we don't see them. But they're there. If we moved one of those fireflies eastward and asked it to compete against brighter fireflies, it would fail, due to no fault of its own. It just has a different skill set than the other fireflies. As teachers, we should respect everyone's individual gifts and put them in an environment where they can use those gifts for the good of the whole.

> *"...we should respect everyone's individual gifts and put them in an environment where they can use those gifts for the good of the whole."*

The collective knowledge built in a collaboration is the most valuable element. It is hard to argue that collaboration isn't a vital skill for our students to learn. I think of skills as a muscle to be exercised. We all have the ability, we just need to build the muscle. We build that muscle by doing exercises in situations where we practice collaborating.

If I rated these ten elements in order of importance, collaboration would be near the top of the list for me. It is that vital. Collaboration is a key element that should be incorporated into every project. This helps to foster this sense of community in your students. They realize they are all working toward a common goal, which is learning, and they begin to champion for each other. The projects also turn out better because of the collective work of the group. I like to joke that if learning were not meant to be social, then Hogwarts wouldn't exist. I mean, if anyone could come up with a better way to learn, it would be wizards, right?

Think back to the synchronous fireflies I wrote about earlier in the book. The Great Smoky Mountains National Park actually has a lottery to determine which families get the opportunity to view the firefly display in the best viewing areas in Tennessee. I believe it is so popular because a quality display of collaboration is a truly beautiful thing!

## Takeaways

### What's in the Jar?

- All students need to feel they are contributing.
- Improv is a great collaboration tool.
- We should respect everyone's individual gifts and put them in an environment where they can use those gifts.
- Collaboration builds community.
- Learning is social.

### #fireflyclass

- How important do you think collaboration is to the learning environment?
- In what ways have you used collaboration in your classroom to find the fireflies of learning?

Students need to feel like the hero of the story happening in your classroom.

# Chapter 6

*Fireflies Need Support to Fly*

**A** - Task is integrated **A**cross different Subjects

*The Firefly Rollercoaster*

"You mean we get to make our own theme park? That is so cool!" shouted Lexi excitedly. She had just had a summer visit to Disney World in Florida and was fondly recalling her trip.

"Can I see the Magic Kingdom map again?" she blurted out, having difficulty containing her enthusiasm.

I was (and still am) a huge Disney theme park fan. Over my years of attending the different parks, I had thought that the Disney customer service model would make for a good classroom. I had read a particularly poignant book by Adam M. Berger titled *Every Guest is a Hero: Disney's Theme Parks and the Magic of Mythic Storytelling*. The book discusses in detail how the Disney model puts each guest as the hero in their own story. Whether it be the queue experience or the multitude of ride details, it is all designed to make each guest feel like they are the hero of the story. Along the same lines, students need to feel like the hero of the story happening in your classroom.

This idea mulled in the back of my mind for several years until I met Howie DeBlasi at EdCamp Magic in 2015. Howie, a huge Disneyphile himself, told me about a project he did where students designed a theme park using lessons from Disney. What better way to teach theme than designing a *theme* park?

# Lesson Elements

### Open the Jars

To introduce the project, I got park maps on eBay from several of the Disney parks, as well as from Universal Studios and a couple of nearby parks the kids were more familiar with: Kings Island and Holiday World. This cost me less than $10. I laminated the maps and distributed them around the classroom. In small groups, I asked the students to examine the maps and look for elements that stood out to them.

"They all have places to eat?" said Michael.

"Yes, they do that to keep visitors in the park. If they have to leave to get food, they might not come back," I said.

"They named all their rides," said Trystan.

"Yes! And do those names have anything in common?"

"They're named after movies?" she answered, a little unsure, as she held up the Universal Studios map.

"Do all your maps have rides named after movies?"

The students looked at their maps and scanned the names. "Some do and some don't," said Andrea. "I mean, we have some that are Disney movies, but others I don't think are movies."

"Interesting," I pretended to ponder. "So, Universal Studios, which is a movie-making company, has all their rides named after movies?" I continued, "but, Disney, which also makes movies, doesn't name all their rides after movies? Hmmm, I wonder why that is."

No response.

"Holiday World," I looked in the direction of the group that had the Holiday World map, "What are your rides named after?"

"We're not sure," said Carrie timidly. "But it looks like holidays?"

"Yes!" I then went into the explanation that Holiday World, located in Santa Claus, Indiana (yes, really), used to be named Santa Claus Land. When they wanted to expand, the natural growth was into other holidays.

"So, you end up with Halloween and a roller coaster called 'The Raven.' Or Thanksgiving and a ride called the 'Gobbler Getaway,," I said.

"Wait, our park has several areas, too, that are similar, and the ride names match," said Gabby as she had an epiphany.

"What do you mean?"

"Well, our group has Universal Studios and it has 'Harry Potter World' and 'The Simpsons'…." she trailed off.

"It seems these parks have a theme," said Trystan.

"Exactly, well-designed theme parks have a theme that ties the park together."

"Is that why they call it a *theme* park?" inquired Maria with a smile.

"Great observation!" I said.

And, thus, the kids were realizing what a theme was supposed to do, all through some guided inquiry.

I then showed them a YouTube video of the line and ride experience for Expedition Everest at Disney's Animal Kingdom. This ride is considered by some to be the best example of ride storytelling in all theme parks. The ride isn't based off a movie or other previously written story, so the creators had carte blanche to write their own story. They chose to use Mount Everest and a yeti as a character to add some familiarity for the riders.

As the students watched the video intently, I pointed out different elements through the queue and on the ride that added to the story. Afterward, we had a discussion about what the story was. Admittedly, this was a bit difficult because most of the students had never experienced the ride, and their only exposure was a somewhat blurry YouTube video. I showed them pictures of the village of Serka Zong surrounding Expedition Everest, and we looked on the Animal Kingdom map to see how that story fit the theme of the "Asia" section of the park.

Now the students were beginning to grasp the relationship of theme to story and also story to ride experience. During this entire lesson, not a single student asked, "Why are we learning this?" The students were curious to learn about theme parks and rides. As I saw the fireflies really sparking, I decided it was time to tell them about their project.

"You are going to design your own theme park!"

## Jars Open, Lids Ready

The first step was to divide up groups. The groups would agree on a theme for their theme park. Once agreed, each group member would be responsible for an area or "land" of their theme park. Then they had to write at least one complete ride story in their land.

Additional requirements were that the groups had to draw a map for their entire park, clearly labeling the theme-related items. Each group also had to build a prototype for at least one of the rides in their entire park. They could collaborate with each other. The prototype should be as functional as possible. I chose this element of the project in order to incorporate some science, engineering, and math into the project. With the problem communicated, the students began working.

"Did you know the guy from the game Operation actually has a name?" Trystan asked me as I made my way around the room checking on groups. "It's Cavity Sam."

"I did not know that," I replied. "What kind of theme park is your group doing?"

"We're doing all board games," piped in Miranda.

"That sounds clever."

"Yeah, Miranda has Candy Land, Trystan has Operation, Maria is doing Mousetrap, and I'm doing Chutes and Ladders," said Andrea with enthusiasm.

"Our map is going to look like a game board," announced

Maria excitedly.

"We're still deciding on a name, though," grumbled Miranda.

They showed me a few of the ideas they had sketched out. I wished them luck and moved on because I saw another group all working independently.

"Hey, Lexi, what are you working on?" I asked, surprised to see her group working individually this early in the process.

"I'm looking up the lyrics to 'LA Devotee,'" she answered.

Confused, I responded, "That has to do with your theme park?"

"Yeah," she said as she laughed. "We decided to do a theme park with all bands or music. I'm doing 'LA Devotee' by Panic at the Disco, and so I'm looking at the lyrics to help me with the story."

"What is the rest of your group doing?" I asked as I peered over at three students lost in thought.

"They're still deciding their music."

"Fair enough. Carry on," I responded, as I began to make my way to other groups.

By the end of the first day, one group was doing an underwater water park based around different major world cities; another was doing a park themed around different decades of U.S. history; yet another was going to tastefully do a theme park based on different wars; and the final group I visited with was basing their park around adventures in general.

As the days progressed, students were incorporating history by researching historical events, science and engineering by determining the viability of their designs, economics by planning the best layout for their park to maximize the balance between guest experience and profit, English by examining storytelling and theme along with research, art by meshing the aesthetics of their park with the theme, and more.

## Closing the Jars

The final product for each group was a map, a ride prototype, and a basic description of their park. In addition, each student also had to turn in a small description of their own area of their group's theme park as well as a story that was portrayed in one of their rides. A Firefly Classroom strikes a good balance between individual and group work. The groups then presented their park ideas and a short synopsis of their stories informally. When I say "informally," it means I didn't assess the presentation as part of the project. It was more a way for the groups to share their work with the class and to practice the skill of presenting a synopsis.

This was also an informal reflection piece. By presenting to the class, they got to receive feedback in the form of questions from their peers. And sometimes just hearing yourself say something out loud makes you realize some discrepancies or inconsistencies in your own work. Students had so many

Firefly moments during this project that the room was always bright and active.

If you are interested in seeing an extremely detailed theme park unit plan, connect with Howie DiBlasi on his website[8] or on Twitter (@hdiblasi) and request his free 279-page ebook titled *Imagineering Classrooms: PBL and STEM Lessons*.

---

8 http://www.drhowie.com/

## Firefly Flying Experience

When students in firefly classrooms gain the ability to fly, we open up a world to them that includes support and connection. When we gift them that ability to fly, we must stress that they should be more than visitors. Our goal should be for Firefly students to be creators, sharers, and contributing members to the world in which they fly.

> *"Our goal should be for Firefly students to be creators, sharers, and contributing members to the world in which they fly."*

I mentioned earlier the eighth graders at my school went on a class trip to Washington, DC. It is a common activity for many schools across the U.S. In our case, every April we loaded all the eighth graders on a bus and drove the 11+ hours to our nation's capital. It was a trip the students anticipated for years and was a very fun event. However, while fun was a definite plus, I saw it also as an opportunity for the students to capture some learning in multiple subject areas. As teachers, we sometimes joked that the kids would have been just as happy to ride the bus around all day with their friends and not make so many stops to see this memorial or that building. But I wanted them embrace the value of the trip by being actively involved in the experience.

# Lesson Elements

### Open the Jars

"You mean the National Mall is not really a mall?" asked Summerlin when she began her research. "Oh man, I was getting excited to go to an actual mall." The class laughed.

"That's a common confusion at first for eighth graders," I assured her. "No, a 'mall' is actually a walking area or promenade between some common element, often stores or shops, and that's what you're familiar with, but the National Mall connects several museums and monuments in DC."

Leading up to the trip, I had the students in groups researching a sight that we would visit in DC.

"Did you know it has 19 museums?" Summerlin shouted in amazement as she read from her laptop screen.

"I did not. I mean, I knew it has a lot of museums, but I didn't know the actual number."

"This looks pretty cool," she informed me as I made my way around the classroom, clearly over her disappointment of not getting to research a shopping mall.

"Did you know the Washington Monument is two different colors?" asked Joey of no one in particular."

"Why is that, Joey?" I asked, offering him the chance to tell everyone a fact he discovered.

"The were building it before the Civil War and then had to stop. They completed it after the Civil War using marble from a different quarry."

Many students immediately found Google images of the Washington Monument so they could see what Joey was referencing.

We also included more contemporary sites during our visit, like the Newseum, the Kennedy Center, and the Vietnam War Memorial Wall, among other. We wanted students to grasp the whole collective of our nation's history.

## Jars Open, Lids Ready

I wanted the students actively invested in the itinerary and not just passive participants. I grouped the students by sites and tasked them to do extensive research to present to the class before we left. This not only gave the students some ownership in the trip, but also generated more knowledge and appreciation for what they were going to see.

As the students conducted their research, they also collaborated on mapping out the stops using Google Maps. To appreciate the trip more, I wanted them to understand the costs associated. So they researched gas prices, mileage, admission fees, etc., and used math skills to calculate their expenditures on the trip. We also categorized the events of each day by main intent, for example, social, educational, necessity (food), and more. Students then factored the percentages of each in order to realize how much time they had dedicated to each. The students really embraced the trip as their own and gave their presentations with enthusiasm to excite their classmates.

### Closing the Jars

The pre-trip presentations weren't the end of the project, though. I wanted them to share their learning with other students and their families. I wanted this to happen during the trip so they could reflect on what they were seeing and feeling so they could bring the entire learning experience full circle. While on the trip, students were assigned to report on their site. At the site they made a short video[9] and wrote up an informal report about their experience. I would then put the video and write-up on a blog for parents, other family members, and the school community as a whole to see. Oftentimes followers would comment and elicit a dialogue amongst others in the community. I supplemented the blog with my own posts for consistency for and audience engagement between the student posts. In the end, the students got a fun, authentic experience that also enriched their time in Washington, DC.

---

9 https://youtu.be/7tTnDAj99_g

## Fireflies Need Support to Fly - Integrate Across Different Subjects

Firefly students need support to fly. They can't experience authentic learning if they don't get all the tools from multiple disciplines. I'm not trained to teach math, so incorporating math into a project was complicated for me, but necessary. If you are in a situation where you work as a team of teachers or are a self-contained teacher who teaches all core subject, then that can be helpful.

This element is another one of those real-world skills that pay dividends in the future. If our students can make content connections across subject areas, their learning grows exponentially. One thing I did when planning a project was to brainstorm with someone from another content area. I would talk to a science teacher or a math teacher and see the project from their perspective. Sometimes a science teacher would say: "Well, that's not really in my standards. That's more for a different grade."

My response was: "Well, how can we make it your standard? Let's be flexible and work with this."

The more subjects that can be captured by students, the more valuable the project becomes. If you can link even small nuggets from other content areas, you should. In the end, our Firefly students get the support they need to fly on to greater things.

# Takeaways

### What's in the Jar?

- Tapping into your interests and your students' interests makes for more passionate projects.
- Fireflies need to be allowed to fly in order to support each other.
- A Firefly Classroom strikes a good balance between individual and group work.
- Incorporating multiple disciplines allows all students to fly.

### #fireflyclass

- How can you find ways to tie multiple content areas into your projects?
- With whom can you brainstorm new ideas in order to expand the content of your projects?

# Chapter 7

*The Light of a Firefly Is the Product*

**P** - *Task involves producing a **P**olished **P**roduct*

*Firefly Efficiency*

The light produced by a firefly is the most efficient light around. Almost 100% of the energy is converted to light. I see that process is very similar to a simple machine.

When a sixth grade teacher came to me wanting ideas on teaching simple machines, I started to brainstorm. It seemed obvious to teach the concepts involved in a simple machine by making a simple machine. If you Google "simple machines projects," they all involve building your own simple machine. Simple, right?

My concern when designing this project for sixth grade wasn't the act of having students build a random simple machine, but was having them understand enough about the process to build a *good* simple machine with intention. To understand pulleys and levels and balance and all the other concepts that go into a simple machine, you have to build them to work and to work consistently.

# Lesson Elements

### Open the Jars

Our first step was to have the students explore simple machines. Therefore, I had them search Instructables.com for simple machine instructions. Instructables is a website where users can upload how-to instructions for just about anything: from a Ghostbusters Proton Pack to wasabi deviled eggs. A search for simple machines brings up hundreds of user-submitted plans for building simple machines.

After the students looked at some of the simple machines, I had them present one of the simple machines to the class and explain how it worked.

"You see, this thing rotates around and drops the ball," said Anden while explaining the machine.

"That would called be a pulley," interrupted the sixth grade teacher politely.

This was our opportunity to introduce vocabulary for concepts or actions needed to understand simple machines more fully.

"How does that even work?" Chad said in disbelief as he watched a video of a simple machine one of his classmates had selected.

"I'm still trying to figure it all out," responded Robert.

"Let's watch it again and see if we can figure it out," I added.

After some discussion, the class was able to discover how that particular simple machine worked using the printed instructions and the video demonstration. The students could ask each other questions and have an open dialogue about simple machines. It was a very low-pressure inquiry activity to get the students generating ideas.

## Jars Open, Lids Ready

I then tasked the students with building their own simple machine. The task they had to complete was to turn off a light switch using three different processes. Students worked in small groups concepting and building simple machines. They tested and retested, asked for feedback from others, and really dug into the concepts.

I could have stopped there and made it a decent project. But that wasn't enough. I wanted them to really work to make a simple machine that would consistently perform. Firefly Classrooms should work for a polished product, and I felt the best way to do that was to share that project with others outside the classroom. Therefore, I had the students document all the processes of the machine into a set of instructions.

Preparing detailed, accurate, and complete instructions was an important skill for students to practice. One of the purposes of having them review other people's simple machine instructions was for them to get an idea of what worked and what didn't work instructionally.

"I liked the pictures," said Lexi, who was a very visual learner. "They helped me understand what was going on."

"Yeah, like the video we watched for Robert's machine," pointed out Carrie.

"Yes, photos and videos help a lot of people understand an instruction better."

The students agreed it was important to add photos and video to their instructions. Which meant they had to build a consistently working machine in order to get good photos and/or video.

"They're very detailed," commented Andrea, the perfectionist in the crowd.

"Good observation," I continued. "You can't assume that some steps are too easy and don't need to be mentioned. Good instructions include every little detail no matter how small it seems."

"Mine made me angry because they left something out I should have known later," said Carrie.

"What do you mean?"

"Well, it said something like, 'push the posts together', but didn't say don't glue them together yet," she continued. "So I glued them together too early and had to start over."

"Good point, Carrie. Anticipating common mistakes people make and noting that is helpful."

Reflecting on the instruction process was a good time for the students to realize what they learned.

"So, how can we identify common mistakes?" I asked the class.

A very long silence. Then someone mumbled, "Do it?"

"OK, how do you think companies know if their instructions are good or not?"

A very long silence. Then a mumbled, "Test it?"

I shot my eyes to the back of the classroom and identified Maria as the source of the mumbles. "Yes, Maria. They test their instructions." I peered around to monitor visual feedback. Students looked a bit perplexed, so I added: "Companies will get groups of people to try their instructions and give them feedback. Before they print thousands of instruction manuals and ship them with whatever they're selling, they want to make sure the customer can follow them."

"Do they pay these people?" asked Michael.

"Yes, probably. Or maybe give them some free products. They're called focus groups. Companies do it for all kinds of products. Starbucks might test a new flavor of drink on a focus group before they put it in all their stores."

"That's the kind of job I need," said Gabby to the laughter of her classmates.

"So I've gotten you a focus group."

"What?" several students responded curiously.

"I got a teacher from another sixth grade class to let his

students review your instructions. They will see if they can build the machines using your instructions and then give feedback on them."

"Oh great, now we have to do a good job on them," said Andrea sarcastically as she smiled.

"Yes, but that's what the focus group is for. To let you know where you made mistakes so you can improve."

### Closing the Jars

The other class (which I found on Twitter) took a week to review our instructions and then sent feedback.

"If I could have explained it, they would have understood it," said Rebecca when reviewing her feedback.

"Exactly. You need to explain it better. You don't have the luxury of being able to explain every detail to each person that reads your instructions. You can't leave anything that needs explaining."

The students took that feedback and revised their instructions accordingly. Afterward, they uploaded the instructions to Instructables.com for others to use. The important part to capturing their fireflies wasn't just building a simple machine. It wasn't just producing instructions, either. It was going through the iterative process and ensuring their instructions were polished. That polished product piece made the simple machines project truly authentic.

## Firefly Broadcast

Given my history with podcasting, it was only a matter of time before I implemented podcasting in the classroom in order to have my students experience that. I discussed in a previous chapter when I had my students do an oral histories podcast. This project was different in that, rather than focus on perspective, I wanted the students to focus on final product. My focus on producing a polished podcast led me to so much learning, that I knew this would be great for student learning.

# Lesson Elements

### Open the Jars

I was initially surprised by how many of my students had not heard of podcasts before. Or, if they had, they only had a very vague idea of what they were. Therefore, the first part of the project was for them to go on iTunes and search for subjects in which they had an interest. Then they narrowed down their search to a few podcast episodes and listened to parts of them. To help them, I showed them how to tell when a podcast was most recently updated, how many episodes a podcast had, and other variables that helped choose better podcasts for their first podcast listening experience.

After the initial podcast inquiry, we had a group discussion on what they liked and didn't like. We talked about audience, audio quality, length, and more. This was different than the classes that did oral histories, because we were now exploring podcasting and not oral histories; however, storytelling was important in both. In this case, students were discovering the concepts that make a good podcast as we were discussing. So now it was time to create a podcast.

## Jars Open, Lids Ready

I knew the skills to creating a podcast, understanding production elements, as well as crafting good narratives, took more skills than most students could accomplish individually, so I decided to pool resources and have the entire class create a group podcast. I took the experience I had with my previous class that had produced the oral histories podcast, so I knew which tool to use, Audacity, and the technical side of making this podcast.

## Head Firefly

First, students auditioned for the role of producer. The producer didn't have to record any audio themselves. Instead, they were responsible to make sure everyone else was producing consistent work and editing together the final product, including transitions.

"I'm good at bossing people around," asserted Grace.

"I know you are, Grace," I said with a sly smile. "Does that mean you want to be considered for producer?"

"Yes," she said emphatically.

Will timidly raised his hand.

"Yes, Will?"

"I think I could be the producer," he said, gaining a little more confidence.

"Tell us why."

"Well, I'm really good with technology," he said. "I think I would do a good job of editing it."

"Have you ever edited audio before?"

"No, but I've edited a lot video."

"OK, anyone else?"

Auggie's hand shot up.

"OK, Auggie, what do you offer?"

"I don't like the sound of my voice and don't want to record myself," she said with a smile. "Plus, I'm good with technology, like Will, and I can boss people around like Grace."

"All good points."

Once students had the opportunity to state their case to be the producer or co-producer, the class then anonymously voted who they thought would do the best job as the producer. In the end, Will was selected.

### What Do Fireflies Talk about?

Producer in place, we then had to brainstorm topics. The objective was for the entire group to produce a segment of one overall podcast. Therefore, they couldn't be random topics put together. There had to be a uniting theme to the podcast. I understand podcasts are supposed to be ongoing, but most podcasters last only seven episodes before they give up, so I wanted the students to have a positive experience and create one good episode with this project. It is hard and takes a lot of work to consistently produce good, creative content for anything: a podcast, a TV show, a book, a comedy show, whatever. It was important to me that this be one polished product from all the students.

Grace weighed in, "I think we should do things that annoy me!"

"Well, Grace, how could everyone know what annoys you? I mean, this isn't an all-about-Grace podcast," I said in jest.

"Well, I mean everyone could do what annoys them."

"OK, one suggestion is 'things that annoy you.'"

"I hate it when you are walking down the street and a

stranger is coming the other direction, and you don't know when to make eye contact and if you should say anything to them," piped in Moira as the class laughed.

"That's interesting, Moira, and I'd like to pursue that further, but right now we're just coming up with theme ideas and not podcast ideas."

"Oh, I know, but I just wanted to share," she said with an adorable smile.

"Can we do music reviews?" asked Mary Grace.

"Well, I want to do movie reviews, not music," said Vacketta.

"If that's the case, I'd want to do TV show reviews," said Claire as she sneered at her friend Vacketta.

"Sounds like we're getting a lot of ideas," I said.

Then Will timidly raised his hand again. "What about media?"

"What do you mean?"

"Well, music, TV, and movies are all media. We could do a media theme and include all those."

"Good point, Will. Already thinking like a producer!"

"Could I talk about media that annoys me?" asked Grace smiling.

"That's up to your producer!" I said with a grin.

"Well, I wouldn't want to do a review, but I'd like to do a parody of a TV show," said Auggie.

"What's a parody?" someone asked.

After a brief explanation of the term "parody," a murmur

started coming from the students. Each one was very intrigued by this idea. A chance to be funny, a chance to "act" like a character, and, in Grace's mind, a chance to make fun of something that annoyed her. After more discussion, the theme was decided: Media Parodies.

# Lesson Elements

 Jars Open, Lids Ready

*Firefly Buzz*

Once the theme was chosen, student divided the segments up and began researching and writing. I provided a couple of quality microphones (Yeti Snowballs) so students wouldn't be tempted to record using their computer microphones or smartphones. The students set off to produce a quality segment, complete with an introduction, Creative Commons music, and professional quality audio in a concise format (to prevent them from rambling, I asked them to produce segments that were between four and eight minutes).

I required students to write scripts and rehearse before recording. This was important to improve the quality of the content, but it also saved time on the production end because there were fewer mistakes to edit out.

As students showed me finished scripts and were allowed to begin recording, we set up a makeshift audio "booth" in a nearby storage closet so students could have no background noise. While I'm not opposed to background noise, because I believe it adds to the authenticity of a student-produced podcast, the students actually requested a way to record without classroom distractions. They had invested themselves heavily in the idea that this would be a polished, near-professional quality podcast.

### Closing the Jars

After recording and editing their own portion of the podcast, with some help from Will the producer, students then shared their segment with another group. The groups listened and provided feedback for revisions. Allowing revision time is important for authentic learning. This editing and revision process was vital for students to capture their fireflies.

*Good enough is never good nor enough*

## *The Light of a Firefly Is the Product*

I don't normally decorate my room with posters. I allow the room to be decorated by student work and Post-it notes and dry-erase boards for brainstorming: a real creativity lab! However, my yearbook rep gave me a poster that read, "Good enough is never good nor enough." I had to hang this poster. Any time a student tried to turn in subpar work as finished, I referenced that poster. I don't want a product that was simply "good enough".

I also had the Facebook motto, "Done is better than perfect," hanging on my classroom wall. These may, at first, appear to contradict themselves. But I challenged my students to find that sweet spot between good enough and perfect. When students take pride in their work, they do a better job. But, not only do they do a better job, they also capture more learning.

Sometimes, this can take a lot of extra time from class. When I first start students in the video creating process, they are rarely very good on their first try. I could say: "For your first time, that's good enough. That will do." Or, I could say, "If we fix these edits and add music, this video would be awesome." The decision there involves time. Asking the student to go back and revise could take another week or more. So, admittedly, sometimes, when we are pressed for time, I won't push for the extra work.

But I make a note to revisit that later, because I don't ever want my students to ever think good enough is either good or enough.

# Takeaways

### What's in the Jar?

- Producing for a "focus group" outside your classroom results in a better finished project.
- A polished product requires students go through the iterative process.
- Post-it notes are a great way to identify fireflies.
- Collaboration amongst students contributes to a more polished, authentic product.

### #fireflyclass

- Where are some places you could get "focus groups" for your students' work?
- What provides your own personal fireflies of learning that you could bring to the classroom?

# Chapter 8

*Fireflies Accomplish a Lot in the Time Given*

***T** - Task is sustained over a period of **T**ime*

Fireflies, depending on the species, may only live a few weeks. In that time, they prepare the soil with nutrients for the next round of offspring, they court a mate, and they reproduce. It is a complex process and fireflies make sure they use all the time in each stage of life to propagate the species. Firefly Classrooms should have projects that are complex enough to be completed over a segment of time while the students learn to be efficient at these processes to propagate learning.

### Fireflies in Space

"You mean we did that all for nothing?" screamed Hunter, an eighth grader.

Other students were frustrated but weren't deterred.

"We learned a lot, Hunter, and had fun. It wasn't for *'nothing',*" said Emma.

In 2015, I became a NASA Airborne Astronomy Ambassador. It was part of an educational outreach program sponsored by NASA and the SETI Institute. As part of the whole process, I had the opportunity to fly aboard the world's largest airborne telescope, known as the Stratospheric Observatory for Infrared Astronomy (SOFIA) for two 12-hour flights.

After returning from my trip, I wanted a way for the students to experience what I had. I had been a part of high-altitude science, and the perspective it gave me had to be somehow transferred to students. I had heard about these Near Space balloon launches from my flying partner Jeff Peterson, and I was immediately hooked. I needed to convince our eighth grade science teacher, Anita Navin, to do it. After much cajoling, she agreed!

# Lesson Elements

### Open the Jars

We ordered the 600g Near Space balloon kit from High Altitude Science[10]. It came with a flight computer (very similar to an Arduino board), a Spot GPS unit, a GoPro mount, a 600g balloon, the tether and tubing to fill the helium, a parachute, and the wooden frame to be assembled for the payload. We had to buy a GoPro Hero camera, a 32gb SIM card (for the camera), a 16gb SIM card (for the flight computer), and the helium. All told, we spent in the neighborhood of just over $1,000 on our first launch.

First, I showed them Nat & Lo's Project Loon video on YouTube[11] to get them excited about high altitude science. Then we Skyped with Matt Berry, an Operations Engineer with NASA working on the DC-8 flight team.

"Do you want to go to space?" Emma asked Matt.

"No," he laughed. "I think you'll be surprised to find that I have no interest in going to space," he said as the students laughed. "I enjoy doing the research and development that will get others to space safely, but I have no interest in doing it myself."

---

10 www.highaltitudescience.com
11 www.youtube.com/watch?v=kQDQ3Ps_-b4&t=8s

The students had a lot of great questions and got to hear of some real-world examples of how high altitude science and near space balloons could be used at NASA. After this introductory exploratory period, we told the students they were going to be responsible for launching their own balloon from start to finish.

## Jars Open, Lids Ready

Next, we put the students into groups and assigned each a different part of the project. A Near Space balloon launch requires a weather balloon to be filled with helium, attached to a payload that contains the computer, sensors for data collection, a tracking device, and a camera. As the balloon rises in altitude, the gases expand until eventually the balloon bursts. The payload returns to Earth to be retrieved.

One group spent their time assembling the payload, learning how to use the flight computer, setting the camera and GPS, assembling the parachute, and making sure we were structurally ready to fly. I added an astronaut Lego minifigure which the students affectionately named Marty McFly.

Another group was responsible for understanding the necessary weather conditions needed to launch, including wind speed and cloud coverage, and then reading the weather forecast to determine our optimal launch dates and times. This seemed like a small role at first, but we soon realized it was critical to a successful launch. Launching at the wrong time could cause the balloon to stray too widely from its flight path, could cause it to hit power lines, could lessen the altitude reached, and many other problems.

One group was in charge of researching all the requirements to launch. They determined our distance to the Indianapolis International Airport, as we were near a decent path and had some concerns about that. They also read charts and maps to determine our launch location in aeronautical terms and also determined our predicted landing location using an online predictor. They then had to file a NOTAM (Notice to AirMen) report with the FAA so we could launch on the day we had selected as optimal.

The final group researched the helium requirements and called helium suppliers to find us the best price and service. On the day of the launch, this group was responsible for filling the balloon and securing it to the payload properly. They also tested the parachute design and made sure it was secure, as it would be needed to bring the payload back to the ground safely.

"Where do you think this is going to land?" asked Cole as we tested the GPS unit.

"I don't know," I admitted. "We hope close."

"This is exciting!" responded Cole as we prepared for our first launch.

The entire school came out to watch the launch. We had

been filling the balloon for about 30 minutes and thought we were ready. I was holding the payload as the students went through their final checks.

"Camera on and recording?"

"Check!"

"Launch space clear of any thing above us?"

"Check!"

Suddenly, there was a moment of confusion. The payload was still in my hands but felt lighter. The students were all looking skyward in disbelief. I felt the pull of the balloon on the payload weaken as the strings dropped in front of me. I looked up to see what all the students were gawking at. The balloon had launched *without* the payload.

We quickly examined the payload to see what went wrong. It turned out one knot wasn't secured properly on the line from the balloon to the payload. ONE KNOT. Therefore, once we got the balloon filled and untethered, in just a couple of minutes the knot slipped and released the balloon. The payload wasn't connected to anything at that point and, thus, as the balloon soared into the sky, we had no way of tracking it. Because of one knot, the balloon was lost for good.

The kids were very disappointed at first. That's when Hunter speculated he had done all that work for "nothing." After an initial point of shock, we quickly reconvened and discussed our options. Anita asked me what a new balloon would cost and, I pulled out my smartphone to look it up.

"Fifty-five dollars," I said. "For just the balloon."

"That's it?" asked Emma. "If that is it, we can all put in a few dollars and get it!"

The mood was shifting. Students were beginning to sound more encouraged. Other students said they'd pitch in to buy the balloon. They were so invested in this project and knew they were so close to success, they wanted to finish it right. In the end, the school paid for a new balloon, and we ordered it the very same day. We all had a good laugh when we realized the next item on the checklist was "Check All Knots."

Launch 2.0 is what we began calling the relaunch. Once the new balloon arrived after about a week, we immediately filed a new NOTAM and began final preparations for a new launch. This time it was a success. Balloon AND payload launched together!

However, the launch was not the end of the project. The balloon flew to a certain altitude somewhere in the neighborhood of 100,000 feet or more and then expanded so much it burst. When payload returned to the ground (and hopefully not in a tree or lake), the GPS tracker iwas used to locate it.

Ours tracked all the way to Jeffersonville, Ohio, some 160 miles away from our school. We tracked it live in class so the students could see where it was heading. In the end, the payload was retrieved and brought back fully intact, Marty McFly and all!

## Closing the Jars

Our next part of the project was to analyze the data we collected. Our balloon reached an altitude of 104,598 feet! The students reviewed all the temperature, wind speed, and other data to see what the payload endured.

In the end, our students had a great time doing this and learned a lot in the process. Their fireflies had been to Near Space and returned to be captured. The project took well over a month to complete, but the students became much more engaged in the outcome, because they had to complete several difficult tasks along the way to make it happen. They always kept the end in sight. And, even when we had a temporary setback, a Firefly failure, they persevered.

## Robotic Fireflies

"Spheros... in English class?" asked Chase.

That was the reaction I got from many of the other students at first, too. They couldn't believe they'd get to play with Spheros in English class.

Spheros are programmable and controllable acrylic balls about the size of a softball. You can use an iPhone, iPad, or many other devices to control the balls remotely, or you can program them to follow commands. Many teachers use them in math, science, and computer science classes. I had twelve of them, and when I was looking for an interesting way to teach some writing skills to sixth graders, I decided the Spheros could be useful.

I was working with a sixth grade ELA teacher, Jennifer Forsee, on building an engaging unit on dialogue, point-of-view, and storytelling. I had recently seen a blog post by another teacher where they used Spheros as the main character in an anti-bullying video. That got me thinking, and this unit seemed to be the perfect fit for this.

# Lesson Elements

### Open the Jars

For our exploratory inquiry, I had the students watch some silent movies on YouTube. Videos that were made by adults and students with the intention of telling a story without audio, similar to the old silent films of the early 1900s. Some were good and some were bad, and I let them explore what elements are needed in a film without dialogue. They quickly realized how important dialogue could be to a story. Instead of starting with dialogue and instructing on how to write dialogue, I decided to start with the absence of dialogue. The idea is similar to the adage that you can't appreciate something until you no longer have it.

After the students brainstormed these elements, I asked them to write a script for a video using the Spheros as characters and no dialogue. The Spheros' actions had to tell the story. Spheros can change colors and "dance" around, they can go fast or slow, but the students really had to explore how their actions and even colors could help tell the story.

### Jars Open, Lids Ready

Once the students showed me a detailed script and Jennifer or I approved it, they could move on to recording. This is an extremely important step. Students tend to jump right into the movie-making process and try to ad-lib the script. This is usually a recipe for disaster. Therefore, it was imperative that we require the students to complete the script first before they could move forward. That way, I could evaluate and give feedback on their script before they spent a lot of time and effort recording. In addition to the script, I required a storyboard or, at a minimum, a shot list. Since time was limited with each group on using the Spheros, I wanted to make sure their time was used efficiently. Therefore, the shot list/storyboard showed me they at least had a plan of what shots they wanted to get for their video. It also gave me an opportunity to discuss cut-away shots and b-roll so they'd be prepared with extra footage to make their video more interesting.

As the students began making their videos, some of them chose to build sets using cardboard and other materials, and that added some really creative elements to their videos. While the students seemed a bit frustrated at first not being able to use dialogue, they quickly learned ways to tell their story sans dialogue.

"Can you make him move faster?" asked Paige to Allie, who was controlling the Sphero off camera. "If he is excited, he should move faster."

"Yes, I can," said Allie. "But he's harder to control then."

"Maybe we could use the 'disco dance' feature, and you could be more excited," suggested Javier to Paige. Her group had decided she would also be a character in her video and play off the Sphero without dialogue. It was a clever choice on their part and something I hadn't thought to do. Firefly Classrooms allow the students to think outside the box on projects.

## Closing the Jars

The next part of the project was to build in a reflection piece. For this, we used EdPuzzle[12]. It is a video tool that allows the user to add audio comments, quizzes, and other interactive elements within a selected video. I had the students upload their videos into an EdPuzzle project and then add their own audio comments explaining the choices they made throughout the video. This allowed them to reflect on their choices deeply, but it also allowed me an easy way to assess those choices. I could listen to the students' own words explaining why they made the choices they made. It was my way of making learning visible.

After the videos were completed and viewed by the entire class, I asked the students to go back to their video and edit in dialogue. This helped them realize that dialogue is an enhancement to what is already in a story, but it shouldn't be the only tool for telling a story. The students were not only realizing the power of verbal dialogue, they were also seeing the importance of nonverbal cues to visual storytelling. This

---

12 https://edpuzzle.com/

project took place over an extended time, but was sliced into smaller pieces so they could complete each complex task in succession. Many times when I assign videos to students, they jump to what the end product should look like without realizing all the steps in between, and they get sloppy or take shortcuts. Holding them accountable to complete each step before moving on takes time, but it is valuable to the entire learning process. This project allowed them to build each step upon each other until the final product was a better product with more learning happening than would have otherwise.

*Fireflies Accomplish a Lot in the Time Given - Task Is Complex Enough to Be Completed over a Sustained Period of Time*

Authentic projects need to have multiple steps, with varied learning opportunities, and should address several standards. This takes time. Trying to isolate one piece out of context into a project can be counterproductive. To engage students, they need to be sufficiently challenged at each step to feel a sense of reward upon solving each task. As they get closer to their end goal, they lock in learning because it makes more sense to the overall picture. If they aren't sufficiently challenged, they don't engage deeply enough to progress forward meaningfully and really capture that learning. Some of my projects can take a month, three months, or even the entire school year, and some as little as two weeks. The more complex the final output, the more levels of learning are sparked in the process. Don't be afraid of the big projects. Fireflies can accomplish a lot in a small amount of time. Those are the projects that really pay the most dividends.

# Takeaways

### What's in the Jar?

- Embrace failure. It is part of the learning process.
- A long-term project causes the students to be more invested in the outcome.
- Firefly Classrooms allow the students to think outside the box on projects and to do things the teacher hasn't even thought of.
- We need to make learning visible.
- To engage students, they need to be sufficiently challenged at each step to feel a sense of reward upon solving each task.
- Don't be afraid of the big projects. Those are the projects that really pay the most dividends.

### #fireflyclass

- What do you feel is the biggest challenge to implementing projects over a longer time period?
- What skills do you feel lend themselves to bigger projects?

# Chapter 9

*Fireflies Decide What They Need to Learn*

*U - Task is **U**ndefined requiring students to define the tasks*

No one shows a firefly how to live and reproduce. Even before they hatch, fireflies are independent learners: figuring out how to eat, how to grow, and eventually how to mate. Their tasks are undefined, but they are self-directed learners.

*Fireflies Don't Spend 100% of Their Time Surviving or They Wouldn't Thrive*

One of the most rewarding projects I have ever done with students is a 20 Percent Time project. The basic definition of a 20Time project (a similar idea is known as "genius hour") is a student-selected, self-directed, passion-based project. I wanted to replicate the Google work environment in my classroom.

The collaborative, autonomous environment that Google has created in their workspaces is genius. The 20Time project was one way I intended to mimic that.

During the project, students are given 20% of their class time, in my case one class period per week, to work on a project of their choosing. Students were given guidance on how to select a project they were passionate about learning and with which they would remain engaged. Students would go through the process of learning more about the topic or idea and present their final project to the class. The biggest value on this project, in my opinion, is that students were learning how to learn. If we want to make life-long learners, we need to give them the skills to appreciate how to learn.

Let me tell you about Katie, because her story is why I was hooked on this project from the very first time I did it. Katie was a fairly typical student. She was bright and capable, but she also had her own difficulties. She was a quiet kid, at least with adults. She was cordial and polite when I talked to her directly, but she rarely asked questions on her own. She was one of those students who was capable of doing the work, but who struggled to finish and turn work in on time.

During the whole process of completing her 20time project, she changed her topic three or four different times. She finally settled on learning to play a song on the guitar. She didn't keep up with her weekly check-in assignments, so it was difficult for me to monitor her progress. I concerned myself more with helping her in other areas of need and hoped she was making progress on her 20Time project.

At the end of the semester, the students began presenting their 20Time projects to the class. I let the students volunteer their order of presenting. Some were excited to be first or second and take center stage. Some waited through the first few until they felt comfortable presenting. As volunteer after volunteer jumped up, I could see Katie making anxious eye contact with me. She seemed eager to go, but apprehensive to volunteer. Finally, we had a moment where no one volunteered and I said, "Katie, are you ready to present?"

She sprang up with excitement, but then, like many teens, tried to play it off like she wasn't excited. She went to the corner of the room and grabbed a guitar case she had brought in. In her presentation, she talked about her difficulty in deciding on her project. She discussed how she decided to learn to play a song on the guitar and the process she went through. I limited the students' presentations to five minutes. At the end, she sheepishly asked if she could play her song even though it would go over her five minutes. Of course, there was no way I could say no.

Katie sat down and began to play a Taylor Swift song. As she played, she also sang the lyrics, which surprised us all. No one was aware that she had a great singing voice, even classmates who had known her for years. She made a mistake part of the way through and had to stop and reposition her fingers. She began playing again and made another mistake just a few measures later. This time, she put her head down in embarrassment. As I searched for words to help her salvage this experience, the class took over for me and began encouraging her on.

"You're doing great, Katie," said one student.

"Yeah, I loved the song," added another.

"I couldn't do what you're doing," admitted a popular boy.

Several other students also added words to acknowledge what a wonderful job she was doing. And the tears began to fall: Katie's tears. But they weren't tears of sadness; they were tears of joy. She finished the song to roaring applause. She was clearly uncomfortable with the attention, but she was proud of herself at the same time.

When I conceptualized the 20Time project for my class, I never imagined that. I thought many of them would learn something valuable to themselves. I hoped some of them would be proud of themselves and maybe even inspire others. I never expected tears of joy and such a bonding moment for my class. When I experienced that moment with Katie in my first semester of doing a 20Time project, I knew that it was something special.

> *"I never expected tears of joy and such a bonding moment for my class."*

Over the years of doing this project, I have had students

do many amazing projects. One student learned how to solve 13 different types of Rubik's cubes. Another student put on a magic show at a children's hospital. Many students have learned about photography, art, music, and politics. I even had one student, Julia, who as a seventh grader won a college scholarship from the Children's Museum of Indianapolis as part of the Power of Children Awards for her project, plus $2,000 to continue her work. Julia put on a fashion show for a women's homeless shelter and donated all the clothing and makeup to the residents[13].

If you want a project that is going to reach and engage all your students, this is a project to try. There are other books out now to help you through the entire process, Kevin Brookhouser's *The 20Time Project* or Don Wettrick's *Pure Genius,* to name a couple. The importance in this project is that it required the students to define their tasks on their path to becoming self-directed learners.

## Experiencing Confined Jars

Can we really understand what it's like to be in a firefly jar without experiencing being in the jar?

---

13 https://youtu.be/0kmfqz0wcKk

# Lesson Elements

### Open the Jars

"They really lived in that small of a space?" Faith, an eighth grader, asked me in disbelief.

"Those are the measurements straight from the book, so they must have," I answered.

Teddy, another eighth grader, had used masking tape to lay out the Anne Frank annex floor plan on the classroom floor. We were reading *Anne Frank: The Diary of a Young Girl*, and he used the measurements Anne wrote in her diary and measured them out to full scale.

"This would have been Peter's bedroom," Teddy explained as he motioned to one area. "And this would have been the living room area," he continued.

It was fascinating for the other students and me. We stood in the spaces and tried to imagine ourselves being confined to those rooms. I had the students do a simulation early on in the book where they had to remain silent for an entire hour while at home and write a reflection on the experience. However, not only silent with their voices, but also with their movements. Like the annex occupants, the students couldn't walk around for fear of creaky floorboard ruining their hiding. The students couldn't flush the toilet or laugh or cough or any of the other hardships Anne Frank endured. Many of them struggled to do this for only the hour required. This is when Teddy got the idea to measure the rooms to scale. The students were really reflecting on how hard this must have been for Anne Frank and all the others in the annex.

For their project, I asked them to create a digital Anne Frank Museum. We certainly couldn't afford to go to the actual Anne Frank Museum in Amsterdam. The goal was for the students to create a digital exhibit that we could share with the world, which captured the experiences and significance of Anne Frank.

### Jars Open, Lids Ready

"Can we do like a radio interview with Anne Frank?" asked Evan.

"Well, I'm not against the idea, but Anne was in hiding," I said. "So make sure it is accurate to her circumstances."

"Maybe she could say she's calling in from an 'undisclosed location'?" remarked Mahayla, making the quotation marks with her fingers.

"Now you're thinking!" I said.

Eventually, the two students did a "Skype interview" (even though they were aware that Skype and video chats didn't exist in Anne's day) with Anne Frank, where one student performed the part of an interview on a popular radio show and the other performed the part of Anne Frank.

"What are you working on, Auggie?" I asked.

"Have you heard of the Sims game?" she asked.

"I sure have!" Now I was intrigued.

"I built the annex, and now I'm putting characters into the annex with traits similar to everyone in the annex."

"That sounds pretty cool," I remarked.

"I didn't put any doors on the house, so they wouldn't leave. Is that all right?"

"Sure. What do you think will happen? I mean, can you control the characters?"

"Sorta. I can make them eat and other things to stay alive, but I'm gonna let them go and see what happens."

In the end, Auggie screen recorded her Sims Anne Frank characters over several Sims days (a couple of hours in real time) and then reflected on their actions. Interestingly enough, the characters reacted very closely to how Anne described their reactions in the book.

## Closing the Jars

For the museum, students made websites, online posters (using Glogster), videos, and Powerpoints. The plethora of projects was mind-blowing. Before that year, I had done a live Anne Frank Museum and had others from the school tour the exhibits. This was no different. However, not only could the students visit online, the parents could visit without having to take off work, and people around the world could visit, too[14].

On the final day of the museum, classmates visited each other's online exhibit, and we shared ideas. Students reflected on how they could have made their exhibits better or different. Having the students define their own product forced them to really explore the significance of Anne Frank. They say you don't really understand something until you teach it to others. The same applies here. In deciding their own exhibit, they engaged more deeply in the content, which led to better learning.

---

14 https://sites.google.com/a/staindy.org/annefrankmuseum

## Fireflies Decide What They Need to Learn

> "Students don't need to be problem solvers, they need to be problem finders."

Students don't need to be problem *solvers*, they need to be problem *finders*. The real problem solvers know how to define the problem. Therefore, when we are too explicit about giving learners the problem, we rob them of a chance to find the problem themselves.

We need to build projects that have multiple solutions, and first require the students to find and examine the problem from many different potential solutions. If we can create an environment where students come together to identify the problem and the tasks necessary to solve it, they can then set out to find a more creative solution. If we tell them the exact problem, we imply there is a correct answer. Our students will be tasked with solving the problems of the future, so let's give them skills needed to be able to find those problems.

# Takeaways

### What's in the Jar?

- If we want to make life-long learners, we need to give them the skills to appreciate how to learn.
- Students need the opportunity to find the problem and define their own tasks.
- Letting the students define the tasks leads to more learning opportunities than you may not have thought.
- Problem *finders* are just as valuable than problem *solvers*.

### #fireflyclass

- What elements of self-directed learning do you think are important to promote with students?
- What skills or resources do you use for your own self-directed learning that could be brought into the classroom?

# Chapter 10

*Fireflies Use Reflection to Maximize Their Light*

***R*** *- Task requires **R**eflection*

The firefly light is an amazing form of genetic engineering. Scientists have examined firefly anatomy to find ways to produce similar bright and energy efficient light. Fireflies have a layer uric acid crystals in their abdomen that reflects their light, making it brighter. Just as fireflies use reflection to make their light brighter, students should use reflection to make their learning brighter.

*Lord of the Fireflies*

"Attention citizens of STA Bay, I have confiscated the plans for your government and am converting the entire island to a dictatorship. I will only return the work you've done if you pledge your allegiance to me," Patrick piped out on the video while also wearing a ushanka hat.

I observed the class closely to read their reactions. I had allowed Patrick to do this with the condition that I could change my mind at any moment if the other students didn't react well. This was one where I really had to keep my finger on the pulse of the room, because it could go downhill quickly.

# Lesson Elements

### Open the Jars

The students were in the middle of a *Lord of the Flies* simulation. If you aren't familiar with the plot of the book, it involves a group of schoolboys stranded on a deserted island with no adults, and it explores the psychological ramifications of what would happen in that situation. My students were tasked with creating their own society. They had to write a constitution, determine how they would survive, how they would build shelter, transportation, and any other necessities for survival. They could do the project as a whole group or divide into smaller groups. By design, it had to be a group effort to be successful.

I had created this whole scenario for the simulation. I told the students we had decided to fly to Hawaii for their class trip. Unfortunately, their plane crashed along the way and none of the adults survived. In the scenario, they were stranded on an island we named STA Bay ("STA" being the acronym for the school's name). I explained to them that they would have two weeks to create their society, which must be able to survive if no adults returned to the island.

## Jars Open, Lids Ready

Patrick came to me a few days into the simulation.

"Mr. Cockrum, I want to leave the group, but I don't want to do all the work by myself. Can I steal what the others have already done?" he asked.

Up to this point, the class was working together and seemed harmonious, dividing the work equitably and making good progress. However, Patrick didn't feel his contributions were being heard. He decided he wanted to break out and start his own government, but didn't want to redo all the work.

"What exactly do you mean by 'steal'?" I asked, intrigued.

Patrick convinced the group to let him hold on to all their plans. He had their constitution, their drawings of clothing and shelter, all of it. "Well, they've given me all their work to hold onto. Do I have to return it to them?"

"What do you plan to do with the work? I'm not saying no, but I want to know your plan before I let you do it."

"I want to start a dictatorship. They can join me if they want their work back, but I'll have full control over all the decisions." He smiled as he thought about having full control.

"And what if they demand back their work? I can see them being very angry..."

"I'll negotiate with them. Maybe I'll give some back if they want to work with me."

After we discussed it more, I told him that he couldn't

physically steal anything, but if they willingly gave it to him, he did not have to return it. Admittedly, I was apprehensive, but also curious to see where this would go.

"I'm not going to tell them, though," I informed him. "You'll need to tell them yourself very soon so they have enough time to still complete the project no matter what way they choose to go."

"Ok, I'll tell them tomorrow in class," he said and rushed off excitedly.

Figure: Sample of student work from the *Lord of the Flies* project

The next day, Patrick came in with a video.

"Mr. Cockrum, can you play this video at the beginning of class?" Patrick asked. "I'm not sure I can tell the group in person. Then you can signal me when the class isn't so angry, so I can talk to them."

Oh, it was getting good. We agreed on a signal, and this allowed me to discuss with the class without Patrick present to get an idea of how they were feeling and reacting.

After the video was played, the class was angry, as expected. Patrick was hiding in an undisclosed location until I gave him the signal that it was safe to come into the classroom. To my surprise, after a very brief period of anger, the group immediately started to problem-solve. Some students wanted to agree to Patrick's demands and finish the project under his tyranny.

"Let's just do what he's asking," said Maddie. "I don't want to redo all that work."

Others didn't want to concede and thought it was best to just start on the work again. "Still, there's only one of him and several of us. We can just divide the work and do it again. It wasn't that hard."

After much discussion, there seemed to be consensus to redo the work, and the students all began dividing tasks.

I let Patrick know he could return to class, and he entered timidly. Although there were a few cross looks, no one said anything to him. Rather than try to negotiate or plead with him, the group just decided to move forward. I quietly informed Patrick what they had decided. He was relieved that no one was shouting at him, and he began the process to complete the project by himself, revising much of the mostly finished work of the others.

As the class period went on, I noticed three girls, Savannah, Erin, and Margie, not really interacting with the larger group. They were being assigned tasks without seeming to agree to them, and they were having some private discussions amongst themselves. Nearing the end of the class, they approached Patrick and quietly started a discussion with him that only they could hear. I suspected what might be happening, but I didn't eavesdrop (even though I tried). I just observed the reactions of the class. Many in the class seemed oblivious that this was happening.

The three girls then approached me.

"Mr. Cockrum, we wanted to see if we could join Patrick's group?" asked Savannah, motioning to the other girls.

"Well, I've seen the group assign you work to do. What will happen with that?"

"We didn't agree to any of the work," stated Margie demonstratively. "They're just telling us what to do."

"OK, I have no problem with you joining Patrick's group. But you need to tell the group. They have a right to know you won't be completing your work."

The three girls huddled briefly then went to the front of the room. Savannah demanded the classes attention. "I wanted to let everyone know that me, Margie, and Erin are joining Patrick. We will be part of his dictatorship."

Patrick sat in the back corner of the room grinning. The larger group was not happy, but some had suspected this might happen.

"What are you doing? That will be more work for you," Bobby said to the girls.

"You guys weren't listening to us, so we decided at least Patrick will listen to us," Erin said, defending their decision, as Bobby threw his arms up in a huff.

"I want to join Patrick's group, too," said Maddie.

"What?" said Wade in disbelief. His group was folding before his eyes.

"Me, too," said Caroline.

After these two students announced they also wanted to join Patrick's group, the coup seemed to quell. The groups looked at each other in a standoff, wondering if anyone else was going to defect. I stood to the side, but ready to quell a nasty argument before it started. After a few minutes of tension, no one said anything, just looked at each other.

"OK, it seems we have two groups," I said, breaking the silence and trying hard not to show my joy. "I suggest everyone have a quiet discussion with their new group and begin working on roles first thing tomorrow."

After that point, the two groups worked without incident

for the remainder of the project. One democracy of eighteen students and one dictatorship with Patrick and five other students. In the end, each group turned in all the required materials.

## Closing the Jars

Some of the students acknowledged they were angry at Patrick for days. Therefore, after both groups had presented their government, we had a lengthy group discussion about and reflection on the project. We talked about human nature (which is a major theme of the *Lord of the Flies* novel), about what caused war, and about many other deep concepts that now had a real-life connection. It didn't take long for students to begin making the connection between what actually happened in the simulation and what happened in the novel. Some students accused me of planning it all.

"While I admit, I was thrilled with the direction it took, I didn't influence it at all," I said.

This reflection was vital to the success of the project. Had we not had the discussion and a follow-up individual reflection paper, many students would not have made the connections and would have just been angry at what happened. Every year I do that project, I don't know what will happen. However, every year inevitably the class divides itself into two, and sometimes three, groups, based on the same human nature elements that plagued the boys in *Lord of the Flies*. William Golding really knew what he was writing!

## Could Fireflies Live on Other Planets?

"Julia and Allie are already finished," stressed Anita, the seventh grade science teacher. "A couple more are going to finish soon, and I need some sort of activity to add to the project."

"You mean like an extension project or activity?" I asked.

"Yes! But I wanted to add a technology component," she asserted. "I've been doing the project for years, and I feel I need to add some tech into it."

I'm not a proponent of adding technology just for the sake of having technology. However, Firefly teachers are always looking to improve their projects, and so this intrigued me.

Anita started to explain the project to me.

# Lesson Elements

### Open the Jars

The project the students were working on was a drawing of a planet's atmosphere. Each student had an assigned planet, and they researched that planet's atmosphere. In the drawing, however, they had to modify the existing atmosphere to determine what would make human life on that planet possible. For instance, one student proposed putting heated water towers on Uranus to supply human life with water that wouldn't freeze. My suggestion for the early finishers was to build in a reflection as the technology piece.

### Jars Open, Lids Ready

I'm focusing on something a little differently in this section. While the "Jars Open, Lids Ready" stage would be more inquiry than reflection, in this instance I am focused more on the reflection piece. That is the element of the project that really advanced it to Firefly learning. In this particular project, the inquiry was in the students researching their respective planet and also comparing it to Earth. I really liked the visual or artistic piece of the assignment and really didn't have a problem with the students using crayons and markers. However, I thought the reflection could be significantly advanced by using technological elements.

## Closing the Jars

I decided to use an augmented reality (AR) app known as Aurasma. Whereas virtual reality (VR) places the user in a virtual environment, AR uses the physical environment and layers virtual items over it using trigger elements. With the app Aurasma, one can place a trigger on a visual item like a photograph, a graphic, or any other thing that remains consistent for all viewers. When a device scans the trigger, some media (oftentimes a video) is pulled up for the user to interact with over the image on the device.

In this project, the students first created a video explaining their drawing, along with an explanation of why they made the decisions they made in modifying their planet. Once the video was completed, using Aurasma they placed an aura on their planet drawing and linked a video. Thus, when the drawing was scanned using a device, the video popped up on the screen and played for the user[15].

Each student then went around with a device and learned about each planet. This particular element actually cycled the students back into the "Jars Open, Lids Ready" inquiry stage. The process of explanation required them to reflect on

---

15 https://youtu.be/D7A6TkfO7qE

the work and the choices they made. After students reviewed each other's work, we had another class discussion on what we learned about each planet. This was an opportunity for Anita to fill in any missing or incorrect details. The ensuing reflection was so powerful for those students, the teacher decided to implement the video reflection piece into future projects for all students and not just the early finishers.

## Fireflies Really Light Up on Video

"What should I make a video of?" asked Tucker.

"Which video of mine did you dislike the most?" I answered his questions with a question, a common tactic of Firefly teachers.

He thought for a minute. "I don't know, why?"

"Well, make one of my videos better." This was a frequent challenge I gave to students. You may have noticed I used video elements in a lot of my projects. With the rise of YouTube, it shouldn't be a surprise that video is an engaging medium for students. Therefore, I decided to take advantage of that engagement and have students use video for learning.

For several years in my class, I have been able to have a near fully flipped class. Therefore, my students were familiar with instructional videos. Every year, a handful of students would ask if they could make some of the videos. At first, I had them help me make the videos, so I could still control the content. As I worked with more students on making videos, I realized they could be set free to do their own.

About that same time, I met Eric Marcos, the founder of the website MathTrain.tv. He had created this website for his sixth grade students to make math instructional videos. The site had many student-created videos, which are very popular with some math teachers. I decided to do something similar, not to copy Eric, but because I realized the value to my students.

That school year, as part of my students' semester portfolio, I required them to create one instructional video. I believed the process of students reflecting on the content of their video would help them to understand the content better. I would also have a collection of videos to which to refer other students if they were struggling.

Students would often ask on what topic they should make their videos. I always recommend to them two things. First, as I did with Tucker, I recommended finding a video of mine that they disliked for some reason. Then I recommended that they remake that video and make it better. Or, second, I recommended finding a concept that they had been struggling with lately and focus on learning that so they could make a video on it. That usually gave them direction, but it also gave them reflection.[16]

For production purposes, we mainly used Explain Everything on our school iPads or WeVideo on Chromebooks. The reason was that it was easy for them to create the video. You see, the important thing was to have them focused on the content via reflection; it was not on learning video production techniques. Only basic video editing was needed. It's important that the technology not take away from the learning. Therefore, even if the videos didn't look highly professional, in these instances I was focused more on the thought process

---

16 https://youtu.be/ZaXcdYUauwU

and reflective learning. I encourage all teachers and students to experiment with making instructional videos. You'll be surprised how much you (and your students) learn.

## Fireflies Use Reflection to Maximize their Light

Reflection is an important component in capturing Firefly learning. Every project should have at least a small element of reflection at the end. However, if you can build reflection into the entire process, that is even better. Reflection should be constantly happening throughout the learning cycle. The reflection not only improves the quality of the product, but it also really makes cognition, and metacognitive thinking, part of the learning process. We all want our students to be lifelong learners. Reflection is a critical piece to helping them to be self-directed learners. They are learning how to learn.

Reflection can be through video explanations like many of the projects in this book. It can be a reflective essay or writing prompt at the end, which I've done several times as well. It can be a survey that you create to get feedback while also causing them to reflect before they answer by using open-ended questions (Google Forms is great for this). Anything that can make learning visible for both you and the student is valuable.

Unfortunately, many teachers skip the reflection steps to save time. In addition, students who aren't used to reflecting deeply will struggle at first. Some students think a reflection is just a play-by-play of what happened, with no observation or discernment. Asking them questions can help them think beyond the surface facts. Once students get practice reflecting, they will often do it without prompting, bouncing reflections off each other or you. That is when you know they've captured learning. Once they reflect their light to make it brighter, they are Firefly learners.

# Takeaways

## What's in the Jar?

- Reflection makes learning brighter.
- Allow students the freedom to explore, but keep your fingers on the pulse of the group so you can adapt quickly if need be.
- Reflection helps students see beyond "what happened."
- Reflection can also be part of the inquiry stages of learning.
- Reflection often gives direction.
- Building reflection into the entire process and not just at the end is important.
- Reflection is a critical piece to helping them become self-directed learners.

## #fireflyclass

- What tools do you like to use for reflection?
- What methods have you found to incorporate more feedback into the learning process?

# Chapter 11

*Fireflies Use All Necessary Skills to Communicate*

***E*** *- Task **E**mploys a seamless integration with assessment*

Fireflies communicate through their light patterns. It is an extremely elaborate process that requires a lot of things to happen. The process is so complicated that even the air temperature can change what pattern they use. The "dance" between the two fireflies is very precise. No skill or time is wasted.

When we design projects, no skill or time should be wasted. If a skill that we are not assessing is required to complete the project, then we need to revise the project. We should either assess every skill or take the focus away from the unassessed skills. Firefly students need to learn the precision of the firefly in order to be successful.

## Fireflies on Trial

"You mean we're bringing Johnny back to life?" Jill, a seventh grader, asked.

"Yes, I suppose we are," I answered. "But only for the sake of the trial."

The students had just viewed the character list I gave them. Jill, a most astute student, had noticed that Johnny was a character in our upcoming mock trial, even though he had died in the book.

"Well, where's Bob?" asked Hannah, referring to another deceased character.

"Good catch, Hannah," I said. "Bob is not being brought 'back to life,' because we are putting Johnny on trial for the murder of Bob."

"Awesome!" many students responded.

# Lesson Elements

### Open the Jars

We were beginning preparations for a mock trial based on the book *The Outsiders* by S. E. Hinton. The book is a character-driven novel from the viewpoint of a gang of teens from "the wrong side of the tracks" as they grapple with growing up. The book is set in 1965 in Tulsa, Oklahoma. In order to really understand the characters and how they develop in the story, I decided to do a mock trial as we tried Johnny Cade for the murder of Bob Sheldon. Since Johnny died in the novel, he is never tried for the murder. However, many of his friends and other character grow and develop throughout the story based on this one event. In order for the students to understand how a character-driven novel works, I wanted them to become the characters.

Each member of the class took on a role in the trial. Most played characters from novel (Ponyboy, Sodapop, Cherry, etc.). Some played lawyers. We spent about a month reading the book and preparing for the trial. Students playing characters were assessed on how well they represented the character based on what we knew from the book. The students playing the lawyers were assessed on how well they reconstructed the facts of the story to fit their case.

"This is an entire class group project," I explained. "Each one of you has a specific role to perform. If you don't do your part, the whole project could fall apart."

As luck would have it, the mother of one of my students was a federal judge. To add to the experience, I had her come to preside over the trial. Not only did this add to the realism, it also added an audience member who was not part of the class. Having someone from outside the class present added to the pressure the students felt to perform well. We didn't keep the trial entirely accurate to a true court of law, because I wasn't teaching legal procedures, but rather character development. For instance, we allowed attorneys more opportunities to cross-examine a witness than actual attorneys would receive.

### Jars Open, Lids Ready

"What if I can't answer all the lawyers' questions?" asked Henry, playing the role of Ponyboy.

"Do your best. If you've read the book and understand your character, the answers shouldn't really be a problem," I continued. "Besides, you'll know most of the questions in advance because the lawyers for both sides will interview you a few times before the trail. They don't want to be surprised on the day of the trial by your answers."

The students spent weeks preparing for their role. Each student took detailed notes about their character traits and planned how they would dress and act on the day of the trial.

"Mr. Cockrum, Marcia (played by Josie) isn't answering the questions right because she's friends with Cherry (played by Claire)," James, one of the mock lawyers, pleaded with me. The lawyers were interviewing all the characters to establish their case or to dispel their opponent's case.

After he explained her answer, I said, "Send Josie to me."

Josie approached very defensively. "That is what I think she would say. You told us to answer how we think the character would."

I gave Josie an opportunity to make her case. After I saw she had clearly thought through her position from the perspective of Marcia and developed her opinion, and was not just being obstinate, I called the lawyers back over.

"That is truly what Josie believes Marcia would say, so you'll have to work with that. I've listened to her argument. She'll keep her story consistent, and you'll have to work with those answers."

"Well, we just lost a witness," huffed James.

"That happens," I said with a smile.

The lawyers continued to build their case and interview the characters until the day the trial came. I set aside half the day for this. Students would arrive at school dressed for their role. Instead of holding the trial in the classroom, I set up a meeting room at the school in the configuration of a courtroom. Our judge arrive promptly. I had recruited students from another class who had not read the book to be the jury. They were to make their decision based solely on what they saw and heard at the trial.

"All rise," said Shea, the bailiff and judge's assistant.

The judge entered the courtroom dressed in her official black robe and carrying her gavel.

"Everyone but the jury may be seated. Shea, please swear in the jury," said the judge.

Shea followed the script. Some of the jury looked around nervously, feeling the reality of the burden of a jury in a courtroom.

"We are here for the trial of Johnny Cade for the murder of Bob Sheldon."

We followed the main protocol of a trial. Prosecution started with their opening statement.

"Ladies and gentlemen of the jury, you will see today that Johnny Cade acted in blatant disregard for the safety others. He carried an illegal switchblade, smoked and drank alcohol while underage, and his careless actions led to the killing of Bob Sheldon," said Travis, concluding the opening statement for the prosecution.

The prosecution followed with their opening statement.

"We don't deny that Johnny killed Bob Sheldon. What we will show you is how Johnny Cade, a boy with an abusive homelife, felt his life and his friend's life, Ponyboy Curtis, were in danger based on previous interactions with Bob Sheldon and how he acted to save his and his friend's life," Hannah said, wrapping up the defense's argument.

The trial went back and forth as both sides tried to build a convincing case while also poking holes in their opponent's case. Both sides did an excellent job, and it looked like the jury could go either way. As the trial drew to a close, the judge gave the jury more instructions and appointed a foreman. I then joined the jury in a separate deliberation room to help them understand their role (without influencing their decision).

### Closing the Jars

After much deliberation, the jury returned to the courtroom. The jury foreman handed a slip of paper to Shea, and she walked it over to the judge. The judge slowly opened it and, showing no emotion, asked, "Jury, is this your decision?"

"Yes," they answered in unison.

"In the case of the state of Indiana versus Johnny Cade, the jury finds Johnny not guilty for the murder of Bob Sheldon," the judge read. The defense pumped their fists in jubilation. "However, the jury find Johnny Cade guilty of illegal possession of a weapon."

"We'll take it," joked Hannah for the defense.

After the trial, there was decidedly less tension in the

air. The students had completed the project to great success. Everyone played their part to near flawlessness. Now that it was over, it was time to decompress and reflect on the trial.

"I thought the lawyers did a great job," said Natalie. "And," she added, "I understand the book so much better now."

In addition to the group discussion, the students were assessed on a written reflection due the day after the trial. Each student needed to reflect critically on their role as well as the overall trial, including what went well and what didn't. This helped the students put their own learning into words.

I did this project eight different years at two different schools. Each year, I was worried someone would drop the ball (or be unexpectedly ill) or something would go really wrong and ruin the day, but it never did. I changed the details of the case each year to keep it fresh, but the story obviously stayed the same. The reason I could do this was because, in the end, the skills needed to fully grasp character development and character-driven novels was built seamlessly into the trial. Just like the fireflies, the students needed to use all the skills I was assessing and no skills I wasn't assessing. I also didn't need a separate test or assessment to determine all the students' knowledge. It came out in their execution of the project and was made visible, not only in their actions, but also in their reflections. Every year, the project was stressful; it was time-consuming, but it was well worth it.

## The Rights of Fireflies

"I want each one of you to draw one piece of paper out of this cup, but don't look at it until I tell you to," I addressed the class as I walked around with the cup.

"Do those have names in them?" Sydney asked.

"You'll see when I tell you to look at them."

My seventh graders were in the process of reading *Lions of Little Rock* by Kristin Levine. This is a fictional book about two teenage girls in Little Rock, Arkansas, in 1958, just before the schools were integrated. These two girls of different races had become close friends by then and had to navigate this world of racism and fear. I chose the book because it looked at the Civil Rights movement from different perspectives. The white students, the black students, the school teachers and administration, and other community members. I wanted the students to grasp how all the different perspectives fed a different narrative for those involved. I also wanted the students to understand what that time was like in our history.

# Lesson Elements

### Open the Jars

"Look at your papers now. It should have a square, a circle, or a star."

"Are these our groups?" asked Carrie.

"Who drew a square?" I asked, intentionally ignoring Carrie's questions.

About half the class raised their hands.

"If you have a square, that is just not acceptable. Go stand over in the back of the room," I said with a bit of anger in my voice.

"What'd we do?" a couple of students asked with confusion.

Ignoring their questions, I asked, "Who drew a circle?" Nearly half again raised their hands.

"OK, circle people, good job. That was good of you to pick the circle. Why don't you get comfortable?"

"Wait," said Andrea, a square. "They didn't do anything but pick a piece of paper."

"I'm confused," said Anden.

"What did you draw?"

"A square," he responded.

"Stop trying to pretend to be a circle. Get to the back of the room," I said angrily.

"We didn't choose the square," Lexi stated emphatically, already sensing unfair treatment.

"You shouldn't talk. You're a square person," I shouted. She crossed her arms in frustration.

"Circle people, you are awesome. Did anyone draw anything besides a circle or square?"

"I drew a star," said both Carrie and Trystan as they looked around, confused at being the only ones.

"Oh, the star people are really awesome," I said as Carrie and Trystan looked at each other and smiled. "Square people, stop talking. Everyone needs to tell the star people they are awesome!"

"You're awesome," a few students said halfheartedly.

Carrie smiled and said, "Yeah, I know."

"It's great being a star person! Isn't it?" I responded.

The square people were getting restless now as I tried to begin a fake lesson.

"Square people, you are interfering with their learning environment. You need to stop talking," I continued as the square people quickly grumbled. "Circle people, make yourselves comfortable. We have plenty of extra seats. Star people, are you comfortable?"

"Yes," the stars said as they giggled to each other, not sure what to owe their great fortune.

"Are any of the square people bothering you?"

Many of the students belted out an emphatic, "Yes." One

student even said, "They need to leave!"

"Square people, move a little bit closer together and get yourself as far into the corner as possible," I said, surprised that they so easily complied, with only a few grumbles.

Finally, Lexi talked back. "This isn't fair," she shouted.

"I didn't ask for your opinion, square person. You drew the square, it's your own fault." I turned my back to the square people as I began my fake lesson again.

"Oh wow," Anden said defiantly. "You didn't give us a choice."

"Oh, now you're blaming me for you drawing the square?" I asked angrily, not breaking character.

"No, we just don't understand what we did?" said Sydney, genuinely confused.

Ignoring the square people more, I noticed Miranda, a circle person, with her hand up. "Yes, circle person, what do you need?" I asked in a pleasant voice.

"Can I lay on the table?" Miranda asked, really getting into the activity.

"Sure, circle people can do whatever they want. Well, as long as the star people don't want to lay on that table. Star people, is that all right?"

Now the square group was really getting angry, so I decided it was time to move the activity along and reveal my true intentions.

"Circle people, how do you feel?"

"Amazing," many of them shouted.

"Square people, how do you feel?"

"Bad," they all responded, still clearly confused.

Then Miranda sat up quickly with an epiphany and said, "This is just like the book!"

An immediate, "Ahhh," spread around the room.

"That was segregation," Lexi said with a spark of energy. Her Firefly was coming out. "People just chose someone that was different than them and told them to stay away."

Now all the fireflies were lighting up.

"You're shapeist," said Manny, receiving a few giggles.

"Lexi, how did you feel being a square?"

"It was funny?" she replied.

"Really? You seemed pretty angry?"

"Well…." she said, a little embarrassed.

"I didn't understand what was going on because you were being really demanding. You had an attitude with us," admitted Anden.

As we continued to discuss, the students began to realize that in this simulation, the square people were discriminated against based on something over which they had no control. The circle people, in turn, were rewarded for something over which they had no control. The students were making great connections to the book. But the star people still confused them.

"In just a few minutes, you guys began to separate yourself

based on how I was treating you," I said.

"We started yelling at each other," affirmed Gregory.

"Yeah, the circle and star people were being rude to the square people," said Meadow.

Immediately, the circle and star people started to deny it, as though it didn't happen. After following this line of discussion, we moved on to which each group represented.

"So, who did the stars represent?" I asked.

"The government," said Gregory.

"The school owners," asserted Chris.

"The wealthy," said Anden.

"All good choices," I confirmed. "They represent a lot of groups. They represent the people who made the rules, those that enforced the rules. People like the government, law enforcement, school administrators…"

Some more Fireflies began to light up.

"Now I want you to think about all these different perspectives, because your next project will require you to look at the issues involved in segregation from the perspectives of all these different stakeholders."

I then defined what a stakeholder was and had the students brainstorm all the different stakeholders we read about in our book. After this, I assigned the students to groups and tasked them with creating a presentation from the perspective of one of the stakeholders.

## Jars Open, Lids Ready

To focus more on reflection than presentation skills, I created a presentation template[17] and had the students follow that guide. The information required on each slide was given to them, so they could focus on content and research. In addition, I created a Hyperdoc with resources[18]. I also went "low-tech" and had the students write all their notes on a dry-erase board so I could review their progress easily each day.

"I don't understand why my group is a stakeholder?" Sydney asked with some confusion.

"You have law enforcement, right?" I confirmed in our one-on-one meeting. "What role did they play?"

"I don't know."

"So, who are the law enforcement?"

"The police? And, um, the government?"

"Yes, police would be one. The government is kind of one. Who from the government?"

Sydney gave me a confused look.

"Who prevented the students from entering the school?"

"In the book? Well, um, I don't know what they were called, but they were the people that would normally protect them. Soldiers, maybe?"

"Yes, they're called the National Guard."

---

17 http://troy-cockrum.com/civil-rights-presentation-slides/
18 http://troy-cockrum.com/civil-rights-hyperdoc/

As I questioned Sydney more, she gradually answered her own question. I had also had them read an article on ReadWorks about the Little Rock Nine.

"So, taking this from a historical perspective or a true event, how was the National Guard involved in this issue?"

"Well, first they stopped the African-Americans from entering the school, but then they protected the African-Americans from violence," she said confidently.

"Exactly! Now phrase that into a paragraph and work it into your presentation."

The dialogue among the groups was very similar. The format of this project encouraged them to have conversations and ask questions related to the content and explore the answers together. My Firefly students got very comfortable with me answering questions with more questions.

After about a week of research and discussions, the students were ready to give their presentations.

## Closing the Jars

I made it clear to the students that they were not presenting just to me; they were also presenting to the other students and should tailor their presentations accordingly. I encouraged all my Firefly students to ask questions of the presenters. Knowing they would get questions, the presenters tended to know the content even better.

Firefly classrooms create a sense of community in that students realize they can and are responsible for learning from each other. Therefore, they are more engaged in their classmates' presentations, because they understand the value of the content for themselves. It is important to note that although I gave the students a presentation template, no two presentations were the same, because the stakeholders were all different. I think that is important, because if all the presentations were on the same topic, the other classmates would quickly disengage. It would be like trying to catch a firefly that never moved. After grabbing it once, they would quickly get bored of grabbing the same one again and again.

> *"Firefly classrooms create a sense of community in that students realize they can and are responsible for learning from each other."*

## Fireflies Use All Necessary Skills to Communicate - Employing Seamless Assessment

The skills needed to successfully complete the project should be the skills you are assessing. If you are assessing something different, then it just doesn't fit. For example, I talk to teachers all the time about teaching public speaking. Many teachers will say, "I have my students stand up and present their assignments all the time." What I tell them is that if you aren't assessing the public speaking, then the students aren't really learning it. You need to give students feedback, give them a chance to improve, and assess the skill appropriately. Just having them stand up and present isn't teaching them public speaking. So even though I had my students present in the last project, I wasn't assessing or focusing on public speaking skills.

As you're building a project, the first question you should ask is what skills or content do you want to assess. Many times I'll come up with a fun project that I am excited to try, but when I examine it against the skills I want, it doesn't fit. Then I have to reconsider doing it. I've even stopped a project midway through that was causing the students too many problems with skills I didn't want to assess. When working on pairing self-written poetry with images, I asked the students to put their work in VoiceThread so other students could audio comment feedback on the poems. However, many students struggled with the technical aspects of VoiceThread and were spending a significant amount of time figuring it out and not writing poetry. I decided it was best to stop the project, discuss it with the students, and revise the project to bring out the skills needed. Which, in this case, meant abandoning VoiceThread. Don't push a project forward just because you put a lot of time into planning it or because the students are having fun. If the assessment doesn't naturally come out of the project process, it isn't a good fit. When it fits, the project will be more meaningful for everyone.

# Takeaways

### What's in the Jar?

- Focus only on skills you are assessing.
- Seamless assessment makes learning clear without extra assessments.
- Keep the fireflies moving, so students don't get bored catching the same ones over and over.

### #fireflyclass

- What skills do you find it difficult to integrate into assessment?

# Chapter 12

*Firefly Diversity*

**D** - *Task has a **D**iversity of outcomes and competing solutions*

There are actually over 150 species of fireflies in North America alone and over 2,000 worldwide. That diversity leads to an amazing amount of differences in fireflies. Firefly Classrooms allow for a diversity in the outcome of projects. Firefly students may not realize the differences until they capture and examine them.

*Building Your Own Fireflies - 3D Design Your Own Product*

"We got a grant to get a 3D printer that will go in the science lab," my principal announced at a staff meeting before the start of a new school year.

"What is a 3D printer?" was the response from nearly everyone.

If you haven't seen a 3D printer, they use a product called

filament (which looks very similar to weed eater line) that runs through an extruder to melt it and mold it into a physical product. There weren't many people using 3D printers at the time, so I was tasked by my principal with figuring out how to use it.

First, I spent about two weeks testing it before I turned the students loose on it. Once I felt comfortable with how it worked (meaning I could actually print something), I worked with our seventh grade science teacher, Anita, to develop the first project we wanted to do. She wanted students to learn the design process, and this seemed like a good fit to do that.

We decided to have the student design their own 3D models and go through the problem-solving process for printing these models. But first we had to have them understand how the 3D printer worked and what was possible, probable, and unlikely. We didn't need them to become experts on 3D printing, just proficient enough to understand what was possible.

# Lesson Elements

### Open the Jars

There was a lot of eager anticipation from the students when we told them they'd get to use the 3D printer.

The first part of the project, I had the students go to Thingiverse.com and work in groups to find templates that tested different types of printing. Thingiverse is a website to which users can upload 3D model files for other users to use for free. Directing them to the website, we asked them to find simple shapes to print. One group was tasked with finding hollow spheres while others had to find a solid cube, a hollow cube, and a solid sphere. Anita also was able to tie in a lot of math concepts into the project as it progressed. Each group chose a template model and then sent it to me to be printed.

After these shapes were printed, the class analyzed their printed products, and we had a discussion on what worked and what didn't work. We also talked about why some shapes worked better than others.

"Our sphere collapsed in the middle," noted Aidan.

"Yes, why do you think that is?"

"It had no support? It looks like the parts of the object that were touching the base stayed together, but the farther it got from the base, the more it collapsed."

The students discovered concepts like printing top heavy items created a need for filler for stability, or that printing items that are "suspended" in space needed supports to be printed. I also demonstrated how "slicing" a sphere in half and printing it as two parts, with the middle as the base, got better results and how the full sphere could be glued together after printing. Then we were ready to move to the design process.

### Jars Open, Lids Ready

"Think about your world around you. How many times have you come across a problem and thought, 'I wish there was a tool or product to do this for me?'"

"Ohhh, all the time," said Chase.

"Well, that's what we're doing here." The students were tasked with identifying a need in their life and designing a product that filled that need. Looks of confusion stared back at me.

"For instance, I wanted something to hold up my phone when I fly. I wanted to be able to prop it up on the tray and read or watch a movie from it hands-free. So I designed a little stand. Sure, they probably sell these somewhere, but that's not the point. I solved the problem myself by printing one."

Now the students were getting it. They didn't have to necessarily invent a new product, unless they wanted to.

I held a group brainstorming session and worked students

through the process of finding a problem and then concepting ideas to solve the problem. Once students had time to do this on their own, they had to submit a write-up of their idea and of the need it would meet. I didn't want them to jump too far ahead in the design process. While trial and error is a valid problem-solving tool, many times a little research can save time on trial and error. The goal was to work through the design process, and the hope was to have a printer-ready product at the end.

I introduced Tinkercad to the students and let them run wild with it. Many were surprised at first that they were designing from scratch. No templates could be used at this point, even if several existed. I wanted the students to create original designs. Once the students got familiar with the tools, they began building their models to be printed.

The students needed to make sure the measurements were correct. The default setting in Tinkercad was in millimeters, so some students quickly realized if they designed it just by eyeballing it on screen, it would turn out much smaller than they expected. All part of problem-solving!

## Closing the Jars

Once they thought they were ready to print, I would discuss with them individually potential pitfalls they might consider. In many projects, I probably wouldn't do this, because I want students to discover those Fireflies on their own, but since the printing process was extremely slow and they only got one chance, I wanted to increase their likelihood for success. I made sure they understood, however, that they weren't graded on the final product they printed, but rather on the process they went through to get there. Remember, they were learning the design process.

Students created hair tie holders, pencil holders, a spork for camping, a multi-page bookmark, a phone charging stand, and more. None of the students' products were the same. Even similar items had different designs. You see, if you assign a project and they all come out looking the same, that isn't a good project. To be authentic, to be valuable, the students needed to engage in the process of creating a product unique to them. The design process is lost if the recipe is already given to them. All the students were proud of what they printed, even if it didn't turn out all that well, because they had invested in the process of making it themselves.

*Firefly Service*

# Lesson Elements

### Open the Jars

Author and educator Rushton Hurley founded an organization called Next Vista for Learning. One of his initiatives is collecting a library of student and teacher made videos, and he hosts frequent contests to encourage young filmmakers to enter. He was hosting a contest called "Service via Video." To enter, students needed to create a short video (two minutes or less) about someone doing service in their own community. I wanted my students to learn storytelling in a visual media and to explore service opportunities, and this contest felt perfect.

I first showed a video about one of my previous students who did a service project for her 20Time project and had won an award for it.[19] After watching the video and discussing some aspects of it, I asked them to look at the Next Vista videos from previous years' "Service via Video" contest.

As they watched and shared, we began discussing the effective elements of a good video. As hoped, students came up with ideas like storytelling, hearing the person in the video's voice (both literally and figuratively), and powerful images and video. One great thing about Rushton's contest is that he

---

19 https://youtu.be/0kmfqz0wcKk

requires students to cite and credit their sources appropriately before being accepted. Therefore, students also noticed how to properly credit whatever they use, unless they created it themselves.

Having worked with students in previous years on video making, I knew a common mistake was that amateur video makers have shots that stay on screen for too long.

"How long should video or an image stay on screen?" I asked the students.

Several answers came out:

"Ten seconds."

"Thirty seconds."

"One second."

The students were clearly just throwing out guesses.

"It seems none of you have ever thought about this," I said. "Let's count out seconds using 'one Mississippi, two Mississippi…'"

All the students started counting to themselves.

"Thirty seconds is a long time," said Trystan.

"It sure is for one shot."

"One second is probably too short," admitted Manny.

"It is quick. It some instances, it can work, but many times it is a bit quick."

"Well, we're going to watch part of a show and see what professional video makers do."

Based on previous informal discussions with my students, I

knew that *Girls Meets World* on the Disney Channel was many of the students' favorite show (they were seventh graders, after all). So I pulled up an episode of *Girl Meets World* on Netflix and showed them about five minutes of an episode. While the students watched, they did a "Mississippi count" of each shot to themselves.

"So how long were the shots on average?" I asked after watching.

"I got like five seconds," said Andrea.

"Yeah, I thought like six seconds," confirmed Carrie.

"Did anyone get a number significantly different than five or six seconds?" I asked.

"No," many said in unison.

"Did the show seem quick?"

"Not really," most responded.

"So, you can see, at least in this instance, most shots were around the five or six second range and it wasn't a quick show. Well, that's the magic number. Most videos keep shots between four to six seconds with seven seconds being the *maximum* you can get away with. Now, there are exceptions, but I want you guys to focus on the four to six range."

> *"Most videos keep shots between four to six seconds with seven seconds being the maximum you can get away with."*

The exploratory process allowed the students to discover, by looking at many examples, storytelling techniques and some technical aspects to think about when creating their video.

## Jars Off, Lids Ready

As students began making their videos, they first had to explore and research people or organizations doing service. Since I showed the students the video on the Power of Children Awards from the Children's Museum of Indianapolis, some focused their attention on past award winners. Other students thought about their interests and focused on those. Some knew a person in their life, an aunt or family friend, who did service, and they focused on them. There was a diversity of service projects and people represented in the students' choices, so they could all tell different stories and use different video making techniques.

Next, I required the students to write a script and make a storyboard. Another common mistake among amateurs is to rush too quickly to record video and not work first through the story they want to tell and what visuals they want to use. The storyboard sketches didn't need to be artistic, but they had to represent each shot. I reminded them of the four to six second rule.

"That's like 25 shots in a two-minute video," calculated Michael.

I was prepared for each step of the process to take up to a week depending on the proficiency of the students. Choosing the service topic didn't take that long, but the storyboard and script writing process did for most students. Then they moved into the production stage. There are three stages to video making: pre-production (brainstorming, writing, storyboard), production (recording video, recording audio, collecting images), and post-production (editing). It was important for the students to work through each process sufficiently to produce a quality video. As they worked on shooting video, I wouldn't let them start editing until they had all the elements collected. I worked with them on shooting multiple shots, multiple angles, finding Creative Commons images and video, recording their own audio, and choosing Creative Commons music.

Most students had all their video shot in one or two days. One group did a recorded Skype interview, so I helped them set that up. Another group interviewed their person in person, and we discussed good questions and how to have an interviewee answer questions so that viewers understood the context. One students decided to tell a first-person story using an animal as the character. The diversity in storytelling was coming out in all the videos.

Finally, the students began editing using WeVideo. Many found the editing to be an easier process because they took the time in pre-production and production so that editing was just piecing together the puzzle they wanted to create. Admitted, none of the students were Steven Spielberg, but their videos were turning out well for amateurs. The important part was that the students learned and demonstrated good storytelling techniques using video.

### Closing the Jars

We ended the process by doing a film festival of all the videos. We did the hoopla of announcing each filmmaker and explaining their story to the audience. Each student was allowed to ask for critiques from the audience and could have the following weekend to make improvements they wanted. We then submitted each video to the Next Vista contest.

In the end, only Miranda received an honorable mention for her video[20]. Others were posted to the Next Vista website, even though they weren't award winners. The students were happy with their work, were more confident video makers, were congratulatory to Miranda (there's that community of learners again), and more aware of the storytelling that goes into all the videos they watch. The diversity of videos, of stories, in this project created many firefires of learning.

---

20 http://www.nextvista.org/anna-the-tiger-exotic-feline-rescue-center/

*Firefly Diversity - D - Task allows for competing solutions and Diversity of outcomes*

---

Author Chris Lehman is quoted as saying, "If teachers receive 30 projects that all look the same, that's a recipe not a project." His point was that truly authentic projects should not be identical for every student. The project has to allow for a diversity in answers and choices for it to be meaningful. If we give them a recipe to solving the problem, all they need to do is follow the recipe. Complex problems our students will face don't have a recipe to solve them. If students are looking for the recipe, as opposed to looking at the problem, they are inadequately prepared to solve problems. By creating projects with a diversity of outcomes, we are allowing for the problem to be solved. If the students come up with a solution that you hadn't thought of, but it solved the problem, that's even better. Ingenuity needs to be recognized. Actually, ingenuity needs to be required! And we only get there by encouraging a diversity of outcomes.

# Takeaways

### What's in the Jar?

- Don't be afraid to learn in front of your students.
- Diversity in outcome gives each student more ownership and pride.
- Students shouldn't just follow a recipe to complete your projects.

### #fireflyclass

- How can you allow for more diversity of outcomes to your favorite project?

# Chapter 13

*Fireflies Are Captured, Not Delivered*

Think of this book as a field guide to creating a Firefly Classroom. You could use these projects as they are constructed to get your feet wet. However, I want you to create your own field guide. Take these 10 elements I have shared with you and use your own skills and experiences to build more authentic classroom activities. I also encourage you to share notes from your field guide. Teaching can be an isolating career. Too many teachers feel pressured to do everything themselves. Just as we want our Firefly students collaborating, we should be doing the same. Sometimes you are the jar and collecting information, and sometimes you're the firefly putting out sparks of learning to be captured by others.

As you build your Firefly lessons and incorporate the authentic elements into them, remember the Firefly Model. The "Open the Jars" stage is inquiry with an introductory hook. The "Jars Open, Lids Ready" stage is when students work through the process of asking questions and finding problems and solutions to capture into their jars. The "Closing the Jars" stage is when students have captured their learning; then they need to stare into their jars and reflect on those fireflies.

This chapter serves as our closing the jar stage. Recall how **WE CAPTURED** those fireflies. I keep the elements on a Post-it note or make a poster to refer back to. And share it with others. Continue to dialogue with the #fireflyclass hashtag. Get feedback from your students after the unit to see if you sparked the **WE CAPTURED** elements you wanted to meet.

The 10 elements are:

**W**- Task has Real-World relevance

**E** - Task is Examined from different Perspectives

**C** - Task is Collaborative

**A** - Task is integrated Across different Subjects

**P** - Task involves producing a Polished Product

**T** - Task is sustained over a period of Time

**U** - Task is Undefined requiring students to define the tasks

**R** - Task requires Reflection

**E** - Task Employs a seamless integration with assessment

**D** - Task has a Diversity of outcomes and competing solutions

Always remember that learning is not delivered, it is captured. Now go capture your fireflies!

# About the Author

Troy Cockrum (@tcockrum) is the Instructional Technology Director for Oldenburg Academy in Oldenburg, Indiana. Prior to his role at Oldenburg Academy, he served as the Director of Innovative Teaching for Little Flower School in Indianapolis, Indiana and as a middle school language arts teacher with St. Thomas Aquinas School also in Indianapolis for 10 years.

Troy was named a Jacobs Educator with the Indiana University School of Education which focuses on innovative uses of technology and inquiry in the classroom. Additionally, he has served as an Airborne Astronomy Ambassador with NASA and a Google Certified Innovator.

Troy delivers keynotes and workshops for teachers nationally and internationally on using technology in meaningful, student-centered integration.

Troy is also a doctoral student at Indiana University in the department of Instructional Systems Technology with a minor in Learning Sciences. His research interests include teacher professional development, blended learning, creativity instruction, and online video applications.

Connect with Troy
Twitter: @tcockrum/#fireflyclass
Instagram: @tcockrum
Facebook: Facebook.com/FireflyClassrooms
YouTube: youtube.com/CockrumVideos
Email: Troy@fireflyteacher.com
Website: troy-cockrum.com

# Hire Troy Cockrum!

When you hire Troy Cockrum, he brings an inspirational, practical, and honest message to teachers and students about using digital learning and pedagogy in meaningful ways. He weaves humor and passion into his sessions that engage audiences of teachers and students alike. He has delivered keynotes and workshops around the world and would be thrilled to bring a custom presentation to your school, district, or event.

www.ingramcontent.com/pod-product-compliance
Lightning Source LLC
Chambersburg PA
CBHW020410080526
44584CB00014B/1257